# Transformed

## A Journey to Daily Spiritual Growth

## LENA NEWBY

Copyright © 2022 Lena Newby

Scripture quotations marked "AMP" are taken from the Amplified® Bible, Copyright © 1954, 1958, 1962, 1964, 1965, 1987 by The Lockman Foundation. Used by permission. Scripture quotations marked "NASB" are taken from the New American Standard Bible®, Copyright © 1960, 1962, 1963, 1968, 1971, 1972, 1973, 1975, 1977, 1995 by The Lockman Foundation. Used by permission. No part of this document may be reproduced or transmitted in any form or by any means, electronic, mechanical, photocopying, recording, or otherwise, without prior written permission of the author.

TRANSFORMED
*A Jourey to Daily Spiritual Growth*

LENA NEWBY
lenanewby7@gmail.com

ISBN 978-1-943342-66-2

Printed in the USA.
All rights reserved

Published by: Destined To Publish | Flossmoor, Illinois
www.DestinedToPublish.com

# *Dedication*

To the One and Only True God, my Lord and Savior,
who is the Power that works in me to transform me and
my life day by day!
You, Lord, are Marvelous!

To my mother, who taught me to love God with all
my heart, all my mind, and all my soul with the
beautiful light and life she
lived every day.

To my children, David and Leah, who provoke me to think better,
love better, and believe better.
To my family and friends, who have loved and supported me
unconditionally through thick and thin!
Thank you for the love and support you all have given to me.

*"And do not be conformed to this world (any longer with its superficial values and customs), but be transformed and progressively changed (as you mature spiritually) by the renewing of your mind (focusing on godly values and ethical attitudes), so that you may prove (for yourselves) what the will of God is, that which is good and acceptable and perfect (in His plan and purpose for you)." (Romans 12:2 NASB)*

# Contents

Day 1 .................................................................................... 13

Day 2 .................................................................................... 15

Day 3 .................................................................................... 17

Day 4 .................................................................................... 19

Day 5 .................................................................................... 21

Day 6 .................................................................................... 23

Day 7 .................................................................................... 26

Day 8 .................................................................................... 28

Day 9 .................................................................................... 30

Day 10 .................................................................................. 32

Day 11 .................................................................................. 34

Day 12 .................................................................................. 36

Day 13 .................................................................................. 38

Day 14 .................................................................................. 40

Day 15 .................................................................................. 42

Day 16 .................................................................................. 44

Day 17 .................................................................................. 46

Day 18 .................................................................................. 48

Day 19 .................................................................................. 50

| | |
|---|---|
| Day 20 | 52 |
| Day 21 | 54 |
| Day 22 | 56 |
| Day 23 | 58 |
| Day 24 | 60 |
| Day 25 | 62 |
| Day 26 | 64 |
| Day 27 | 66 |
| Day 28 | 68 |
| Day 29 | 70 |
| Day 30 | 72 |
| Day 31 | 74 |
| Day 32 | 76 |
| Day 33 | 78 |
| Day 34 | 80 |
| Day 35 | 82 |
| Day 36 | 85 |
| Day 37 | 87 |
| Day 38 | 89 |
| Day 39 | 91 |
| Day 40 | 93 |
| Day 41 | 95 |
| Day 42 | 97 |
| Day 43 | 99 |

Day 44 .................................................................................. 101

Day 45 .................................................................................. 103

Day 46 .................................................................................. 105

Day 47 .................................................................................. 108

Day 48 .................................................................................. 110

Day 49 .................................................................................. 112

Day 50 .................................................................................. 114

Day 51 .................................................................................. 116

Day 52 .................................................................................. 118

Day 53 .................................................................................. 120

Day 54 .................................................................................. 122

Day 55 .................................................................................. 124

Day 56 .................................................................................. 127

Day 57 .................................................................................. 129

Day 58 .................................................................................. 131

Day 59 .................................................................................. 133

Day 60 .................................................................................. 135

Day 61 .................................................................................. 137

Day 62 .................................................................................. 139

Day 63 .................................................................................. 141

Day 64 .................................................................................. 143

Day 65 .................................................................................. 145

Day 66 .................................................................................. 147

Day 67 .................................................................................. 149

Day 68 .................................................................................... 151

Day 69 .................................................................................... 153

Day 70 .................................................................................... 155

Day 71 .................................................................................... 157

Day 72 .................................................................................... 159

Day 73 .................................................................................... 161

Day 74 .................................................................................... 163

Day 75 .................................................................................... 165

Day 76 .................................................................................... 167

Day 77 .................................................................................... 169

Day 78 .................................................................................... 171

Day 79 .................................................................................... 173

Day 80 .................................................................................... 175

Day 81 .................................................................................... 177

Day 82 .................................................................................... 180

Day 83 .................................................................................... 182

Day 84 .................................................................................... 184

Day 85 .................................................................................... 186

Day 86 .................................................................................... 188

Day 87 .................................................................................... 190

Day 88 .................................................................................... 192

Day 89 .................................................................................... 194

Day 90 .................................................................................... 196

Day 91 .................................................................................... 198

Day 92 .................................................................... 200

Day 93 .................................................................... 202

Day 94 .................................................................... 204

Day 95 .................................................................... 206

Day 96 .................................................................... 208

Day 97 .................................................................... 210

Day 98 .................................................................... 212

Day 99 .................................................................... 214

Day 100 .................................................................. 216

# Day 1

Read: *Psalm 23:1–3*

*"He leads me beside the still and restful waters."*

## "Good Shepherd"

In this scripture passage, David calls the Lord his Shepherd to feed and guide him. He says that the Lord leads him to a place of peace and rest. The world and its ways clamor at us 24/7, and produce constant movement. It's called chaos and its yoke upon our shoulders creates commotion, agitation, and a constant sense of "go." This is the working of Satan and the results of his presence at work. Peace and rest are the Presence that Jesus and His Spirit create. Matthew 11:22 says, *"Come unto me all you that labor and are heavy-laden and over-burdened, and I will cause you to rest."* The key in this passage is that we have got to "come." Resting in Jesus is a choice! We have a choice to remain weighed down by the cares of the world and all that it places on our shoulders, or to choose the rest that comes from the yoke of Christ as our Good Shepherd. We will wear one yoke or the other. The world's yoke will bring upset and agitation, Jesus' yoke will bring peace and rest. Choose your yoke and choose wisely because your soul and mind will be affected by your choice.

*Come to Rest!*

## Matthew 11:28

*Father, so often I am running to and from with the business of life. I repent for being too busy to enter into the rest that You have not only provided but have called me to. Make me wise, discerning, and alert to the ways of this world and its snare to steal my peace and keep me in constant movement. Help me to make the time to come to You to be fed, and to be guided by Your Spirit. I choose to take Your yoke upon me, and I receive now the peace, calm, tranquility, and rest that Jesus gives. In Jesus' Name, Amen.*

# Day 2

Read: *Psalm 109:1-5*

*"In return for my love they are my adversaries, but I resort to prayer."*

## "Bless to Be Blessed"

People can be so mean! In our relationships, we expect people to love us, appreciate us, and be kind and gracious to us. This is sadly more often not the case. We as Christians are commanded to love others, while others are harsh, hard, and abusive towards us. We are not supposed to retaliate when attacked, we are not supposed to avenge ourselves when talked about, and we are not supposed to hate back when we are clearly hated! To this, we might say, "Wow. Really God?" Submitting to God's command to walk in love is impossible to do without God, and without another recourse! David gives us that recourse—*prayer*! David's response to the things done against him by his enemy is this: *"But I resort to prayer."* This statement from a known, skilled, and accomplished warrior is definitely food for thought!

We are to pray as another recourse to adversarial situations. We must develop a strong prayer life on a daily basis so that in times when reviling and abuse occurs, we are skilled and disciplined to pray instead of retaliating. *"Do not repay evil for evil, or insult for insult. On the contrary, repay evil with blessing, for to this you were called so that you may inherit a blessing."* (1 Peter 3:9). Prayer blesses your enemy, but when you comply to God's command to pray for your enemy, you will find that prayer also blesses you! It is better to be in God's will on this matter than in God's way. *"Vengeance is mine, I will repay, says the Lord."*

*Prayer, another recourse!*

## MATTHEW 5:43–44

*Father, I need help to pray instead of retaliating when evil rises up against me. My first response, I confess, is to get even and bring justice to myself! This is not Your way but mine, and I repent, and ask for forgiveness. I ask that Your Holy Spirit aid me in my emotions, and give me the mind of Christ. Deliver my mind, soften my heart, and grant to me the ability to yield to Your instruction. Grace me to bless my enemies, and resort to prayer! In Jesus' Name, Amen.*

# Day 3

Read: *Jeremiah 30:10–22*

*"For I am with you, says the Lord, to save you"*

## "His Intent"

It is always God's deepest desire to restore us. Even when sins have abounded, are abundantly perverse, and are "glaringly innumerable." God does have to chastise us, but he still wants to restore health to us. To the lost, rejected, unloved, and uncared for, he desires to accept, enfold, and embrace with his love, mercy, and grace. God's intentions towards us are noble and honorable! In our worst state, God's desire is to heal our wounds from his chastisement, save our souls, and restore us to fellowship with him.

God has designed eternity with us in mind. He is so committed to us spending eternity with Him, that He sent Himself to pay the price for His agenda to be implemented into this world system. Jesus came to earth to carry out the Father's plan to assure our salvation, and access into eternity in heaven. Jesus is God's gift of grace for salvation, restoration, and healing from sin, and sin's penalty of death. It is through Jesus that we can be forgiven and restored to health and wholeness. This is forever God's intent for us!

*Believe His intentions.*

## JOHN 3:16–17

*Father, I thank You that Your intentions towards me are noble, honorable, and true. I thank You for the grace that comes through Jesus Christ, Your provision for my salvation, restoration, and health. You are the Restorer of my soul. In Jesus' Name, Amen.*

# Day 4

Read: *Isaiah 55:8–9*

*"For My thoughts are not your thoughts, neither are your ways My ways says the Lord."*

## "Doors of Opportunity"

As believers, we forget that we are not always thinking correctly. We must remember that God tells us in His Word that our thinking can be off. Every door of opportunity is not a door from the Lord! Some doorways are opportunities to satisfy selfish desires, selfish motives, and self-centered pleasures. This is not the good old path of God and His righteousness! Let us pray for the mind of Christ and His way(s) so we will be able to know what is His good, perfect, and acceptable will for our life. There are some doors that we just need to close! *"There is a way that seems right to a man and appears straight before him, but at the end of it is the way of death"* (Proverbs 16:25).

*Sin has opportunities too!*

## *Proverbs 16:25*

*Father, I repent for all my selfish desires. For having a sinful nature and appetite for pleasures. You have told me to love not the world, nor the things in the world—the lust of the flesh, the lust of the eye, and the pride of life. I ask that You forgive me, cleanse me, and redeem me once again to seek Your kingdom and to be satisfied with the joy of my salvation. Grant me discernment when opportunities arise for me and allow me to seek You and Your wisdom before taking all opportunities presented to me. In Jesus' Name, Amen.*

# Day 5

Read: Acts 23:9–14

*"And (that same) following night the Lord stood beside Paul and said, 'Take courage.'"*

## "Faithful Witness"

The scripture says that God stood by Paul and told him to have courage, and that he had been a faithful witness to Him in Jerusalem. He also told Paul that he would also have to witness of Him in Rome. Immediately after God's encouragement, forty men fasted from food and drink, and came together in an oath to plot to kill Paul. This conspiracy was in addition to him already being in prison. These men had bonded in unity and a curse to take Paul's life, but God was with Paul! God was there to give Paul encouragement, direction, and more importantly, affirmation. We can learn from this passage that there is struggle in ministry. We also see that people will bond together in a commitment to fast and curse to do you harm because you stand as a faithful witness to Christ.

Effective witnessing will bring struggle and persecution. It will stir evil men and women to plot and plan your demise, but we can take heart in knowing God is right there with us. He is trusting us and has confidence in us to continue to stand for Him. If we will just be still and listen for His voice of affirmation and encouragement in the struggle, we can gain strength, peace, and courage to continue being faithful witnesses to Jesus. Now ask yourself, can God trust you with your assignment?

*Faithful or not?*

## LUKE 16:10

*Father, I take courage today to continue to obey and follow Your leading. Strengthen me to face every trial and to not be fearful and intimidated by abuse, hardship, and persecution! Give me boldness to be a faithful witness to You, in every circumstance. In Jesus' Name, Amen.*

# Day 6

Read: *Luke 23:1–24*

*"And they began to accuse Him."*

## "Mature Love"

Merriam-Webster.com states that "slander is to make a false spoken statement that causes people to have a bad opinion of someone." Jesus was slandered by his own religious community and when His time had come to fulfill God's purpose for Him, He was betrayed by one of the very men He had chosen to be one of His disciples. He made Judas His treasurer, loved him as a friend, imparted Truth to him, and yes, washed his feet along with the other men he had called to follow Him. The religious leaders and the people cried out to crucify Him! After all this, Jesus still made His way to the cross! Jesus didn't allow the betrayal of a close friend to stop the Father's plan for His life; Jesus did not allow the malicious slander from people, nor the cry to kill Him cause Him to abort His mission.

Jesus is our example of how to deal with malicious slander and betrayal from people. This includes the people we love, have helped and supported, and the people that are supposed to love us. We are to remain in a position of love. God's love in us for those that defame our character must remain active! Through the fruit of the Holy Spirit working in us, we can love the slanderer, and we can forgive the betrayer. We can decide to continue to lay down our lives, pick up our cross, and follow Jesus' example. Love is perfected in us when we choose to love. "God is love and he who dwells in love and continues in love dwells and continues in God, and God dwells and continues in him" (John 4:12). It is the love of God for you, and in you, that will keep you from retaliating to those you know are deliberately and maliciously slandering your name. Stay in position and continue to make your way to God's destiny for you. There is a crown of victory that awaits you! Do not get sidetracked by the slander, do not fold and lose heart by the betrayal ... stay rooted and grounded in the love of God. Let love mature in you!

*Love your enemies.*

## Luke 6:35–36

*Father, this is a hard thing You command, but I want to please You. I want to obey You, and I want to follow You. Grant me a willing spirit and a mind submitted to the ways of love. You said I am only a lot of noise if I cannot love. I choose the more excellent way, and I ask that through the power of Your Holy Spirit, You empower me and strengthen me to forgive, and continue in love no matter what circumstance I find myself in. Through Christ Jesus, I can do all things! I thank You for Your help, support, encouragement, and love that helps me rise to victory! In Jesus' Name, Amen.*

# Day 7

Read: *Genesis 13:6–18*

*"The Lord said to Abraham after Lot had left him, 'Lift up now your eyes and look.'"*

## "What God Has for You, Is for You"

Strife is the opposite of peace. We see here in this passage that Lot and Abram had to separate due to strife between their herdsmen. It is interesting that Abram took Lot with him when he left Ur. Lot would have had nothing without Abram, yet when Abram told him to choose which way he would go so they could separate, Lot chose the best part of the land. Lot looked at the land and chose the land that would benefit him! What a selfish, self-centered way to treat someone who has helped to make you wealthy. Lot would not have had the wealth he had if it had not been for Abram. Abram, in contrast, allowed Lot to take the best land, and he took what was left.

It appears that Lot ended up better off than Abram, but that is not the case. When we choose the way of peace, consider others better than ourselves, and obey God in his leading of us, we stand to gain far more than it appears that we are losing. There are times in our lives when we have to cut our losses in order to facilitate peace. We must separate ourselves from strife, contention, and people that have attached themselves to us and who would selfishly steal the blessings and benefits God intended for us. God prospered Abram far greater after his separation from Lot. If we take the low road to keep the peace, God can and will increase us above and beyond what we have given up to those who thought they were taking the best part of what belonged to us!

*Live at Peace.*

# Romans 12:18

*Father, You have said in Your Word that as far as it depends on me, I am to live at peace with everyone. Lord, I repent of strife, for being the cause of strife, and for participating in strife. Cleanse me this day from the spirit of confusion, which opens the door of contention, discord, and strife. I ask for Your Peace to work peace in me, and I ask for the grace needed to be a peace-maker. I thank You that Your Peace removes all disturbances, agitating passions, and moral conflicts in my heart, mind, and soul. In Jesus' Name, Amen.*

# Day 8

Read: *Psalm 107:8-9*

*"For He satisfies the longing soul and fills the hungry soul with good."*

## "Certain Something"

God has a purpose and a plan for all of us. It is his desire that we accept His plan. We want success and a sense of peace for ourselves but most times we don't know how to get there. We spin our wheels wondering if what we are doing is going to bring us the contentment we hope and long for. We get to the end of a thing and realize we are still not content!

We recognize yet again that true contentment can only be in, and come from the Peace-Giver, and True Comforter! Nothing we can gain, nothing we can do, nothing we can obtain can fill the heart of a true lover of God. Oh, things may give us pleasure for a season, and accomplishments may make us happy momentarily, but those things will soon lose their power, and we will end up right back to needing that certain "something." When that moment comes, and it will come, just remember to return to "the Someone" who will always have what we really need to keep us content—Jesus and His Spirit of hope, comfort, and contentment. He is always one prayer away!

*Something to remember*

## Psalm 103:2

*Father, forgive my wanderings, I realize my heart may stray away from You by what this world constantly puts in my face, but my desire is to stay in tune with and connected with You, my source of peace and true contentment. Restore me to the gift of my salvation! I am made aware again today that the "something" I long for is always going to be YOU! Thank You, Lord, for reminding me ... again. In Jesus' Name, Amen.*

# Day 9

Read: *Psalm 54*

*"Judge and vindicate me by Your mighty strength and power."*

## "Wisdom Calls"

It is an act of wisdom to cry out to God for help! Life brings many challenges and troubles, and much adversity. David, in this passage, is on the run and hiding from Saul; the Ziphites went to Saul and told him that David was hiding among them. David's back was against the wall, and he had no one he could even trust that would help him. Life can be this way for us sometimes, and to make it through our trouble and trial, we must cry out to God to save us! Recognizing that our enemy(s) are too strong for us and calling on God's help is humbling ourselves, admitting our need for His help, and putting our trust, hope, and faith in the One who is able to deliver us out of all our trouble(s). A wise man or woman seeks out God's help in good times and in bad times.

Cry out to God, whatever the need may be. He is able to save and deliver through His mighty strength and power! Let Him judge and vindicate on your behalf! Focus on Him and what He is able to do. Demonstrate your total trust in Him as you wait for His hand of deliverance by lifting up freewill offerings of sacrifice, thanks, and praise continually to His Name!

*Ask for help.*

## Psalm 7:1

*Father, I cry out to You today for help in my situation. I need Your strength and power to deliver me out of my trouble(s). Vindicate me and uphold my life by Your righteousness. I repent for trying to do it on my own and maybe even for not trusting You to move on my behalf. I put my trust in You now! I wait in expectation for Your hand to move for me. In Jesus' Name, Amen.*

# Day 10

Read: *1 Peter 3:8–12*

*"For know that to this you have been called."*

## "Practice Change"

God is not in our tit-for-tat! It's easy and it's comfortable to do to others as they have done to us; the angry, vindictive and judgmental person will go further and do worse to the person when paying that person back! This seems good, right, and fitting, and it sure makes us feel better! But the Truth is clear: *"Never return evil for evil or insult for insult (scolding, tongue lashing berating), but on the contrary bless them."* Lord, really, never! OMG! How do we even embrace this concept? We must remember to focus on His goals for all of us, which is transformation into the image of His Son, and reach higher!

Practicing following God's instruction is where we begin to make changes. If we are willing and obedient to His instruction to not return evil for evil, there is blessing for us as His heirs, but if we refuse and disregard His way, we bring a curse upon ourselves. We get to choose how we will behave! Lord, help us want to do right, *"for to this we have been called."*

*Observe His statutes.*

## Psalm 119:5

*Father, I have often responded in an evil manner to evil. Forgive my immaturity and lack of self-control. I ask for the help of Your Holy Spirit to bring my attitude and behavior under Your control. Fill me with the fruit of Your Spirit. I commit my way to You, Lord, and receive your grace to respond in a righteous manner to evil. I thank You for Your power to overcome evil with good. In Jesus' Name, Amen.*

# Day 11

Read: *Exodus 14:1–14*

*"The Lord will fight for you, and you shall hold your peace and remain at rest."*

## "Act in Faith"

God's instructions to the Israelites in this passage was for them to hold their peace and remain in a place of rest, that He would be fighting this battle for them. When we find ourselves stuck between "a rock and a hard place," we can become fearful and upset. We begin to complain, and we begin to speak wrong. We rehearse the problem with negativity, indulge in self-pity, nurse our doubt and unbelief, and begin to talk in an unprofitable manner. All these things are actions that do not reflect a place of rest and peace. We say that we trust God, but all of our actions say that we do not. Our life and actions need to reflect the faith we say we possess.

Faith speaks! We are going to say something! We must begin to develop and cultivate a positive confession about what God has spoken to us. What God has instructed and promised, He will do if we believe it, say it, and obey it. When He tells us, "I've got this, receive it, believe it, and say it out loud!" Remember, *"faith is the substance of things hoped for,"* we are not going to see it! It is not evident at the moment, but God will bring what He has promised to pass!

*Act sure.*

## Hebrews 11:1

*Father, forgive me for doubt and unbelief! I repent of a negative confession. I say I believe You, and that I trust You, but I recognize that my actions are far from it! My faith has not been carried out in a way that pleases You. I want to be a person of genuine faith. Help my actions to match what I say I believe. Help me, Lord, to speak in faith, and act in faith. In Jesus' Name, Amen.*

# Day 12

Read: *Romans 15:13*

*"May the God of hope so fill you with joy and peace in believing (through the experience of your faith)."*

## "Abiding Joy"

Our joy must come from the Source of joy. Joy is not found in family, friends, money, possessions, a job, or relationships. These things make us happy, but lasting joy, the kind of joy we need to face every day with hope, positivity, and purpose, must come from the Lord! Joy sought for from any other source will be transient. Transient joy can be taken away from us by circumstances. But the joy that comes from being aware and mindful of God's favor and protection over us is the abiding joy of the Lord! God's abiding joy cannot be taken away from us. The world does not give this kind of joy, but the world will try and take God's joy from us. We have to hold onto to the lasting joy of the Lord and refuse to give it up for mere happiness. Joy strengthens us, and we need the joy of the Lord to live each day joyfully!

*There is joy for the upright in heart.*

## Psalm 97:11

*Father, forgive me for not recognizing my dependency on people, circumstances, and material things as a source of joy. I desire abiding joy that comes specifically from You. I acknowledge the grace and mercy that is found in salvation, and I accept its free gift. Fill me today with the joy that comes from Your Spirit. I thank You and praise You! In Jesus' Name, Amen.*

# Day 13

Read: *Matthew 26:6–15*

*"She has done a noble (praiseworthy and beautiful) thing to Me."*

## "Wasteful Worship"

There is a worship that we have that is just for the Lord alone. We must be careful that in all our serving, we do not let others take what we want and desire to give to the Lord. This perfume belonged to this woman, and it was hers to give to whomever she desired. The scripture says the disciples were indignant and called her worship of her Lord "a waste." The disciples felt that the perfume would be of better use to be sold, and the funds given to the poor. While their suggestion might have been a good idea, it was not their perfume, it was not their decision to make, and they certainly were not the object of the devotion that the precious perfume was poured upon. It is interesting that immediately after the act of this woman and Jesus' response that it was fitting to be poured on Him, Judas Iscariot went to the chief priest to betray Jesus. It is obvious that Judas was provoked by the loss of money! Remember, Judas was the treasurer, and he was stealing from that treasury.

Those that love and worship Christ as you do, will enjoy and support your wholehearted worship of Him. Those that are betrayers of Jesus will always be indignant of your worship of Christ. These disciples will want to take what you possess and purpose to personally give to your Lord and Savior, and attempt to distribute it for a so-called godly purpose. Be careful that your time, your talent, your anointing, your possessions, and your worship are for God and His purposes, not someone else's hidden motives of greed, gain, and selfish ambition!

*Your wasteful worship pleases Him!*

## Matthew 26:10

*Father, show me how to live a life pleasing and acceptable to You. My worship many times gets lost in serving. Help me to remember that service is to come out of my wholehearted worship of You. Make me discerning of the manipulation of others who would use my dedication and worship to further their own selfish greed, ambition, and ungodly gain. Let my worship and service be a memorial to You, not to man and his agendas. Show me how to balance my personal worship to You and my works of service to Your church. It is very important to me that I be pleasing to You! It is also important to You that I live life serving others. In Jesus' Name, Amen.*

# Day 14

Read: *Ephesians 2:4–9*

*"For it is by free grace (God's unmerited favor) that you are saved."*

## "Grace under Control"

For all man's sin, the Father has given a solution. It is in the Name and Person of Jesus Christ. Through Jesus' blood sacrifice He willingly made all those that accept his free gift of redemption acceptable to the Father. We have free access to a Holy God by the grace found in His Son, Jesus Christ. The scripture says, *"While we were yet sinners, Christ died for us"* (Romans 5:8). Grace is God's unmerited favor towards sinners—that's you and me, for all have fallen short of God's glory, and there is no one that does good, no one!

Jesus did not have to die for us, mere sinful humans. Out of love, He chose to save us from eternal damnation. He chose to be born, to suffer, and be sacrificed in death for the penalty of sin. For making that choice to save us, He was given all power and authority in heaven, on earth, and even under the earth. No man took Christ's life; He gave it! Grace has always been, and forever will be, under Christ's control!

*Laying down our life is a choice.*

## John 15:13

*Father, thank You for laying down Your life so that I could obtain eternal life. You didn't have to do it, but You did out of Your love for the world. Your grace is a free gift to all that choose to believe, and trust in You. I believe, I trust, and I accept Your free gift of grace. You paid the price for my sins, and I am grateful! In Jesus' Name, Amen.*

# Day 15

Read: *John 5:1-15*

*"Do you want to become well? (Are you really in earnest about getting well?)"*

## "Change Your Position"

How badly do you want to be healed? Being comfortable in a situation that has taken all our strength, and made us feel sick and hopeless, is not living an abundant life. The man at the pool was hopelessly sick and helpless. He had been in this condition for a long time. *"Hope deferred makes the heart sick."* There can appear to be no way out of the situation we find ourselves in, but Jesus is able to heal, deliver, and set free despite the circumstance that is trying to dictate our future! Jesus is and always will be our way out of a hopeless and helpless situation! In fact, "hopeless" is where He works best! When we are weak and unable to help ourselves, His strength on our behalf is made perfect. We must decide if we really want His intervention and make no more excuses for where we are.

We can make the decision to change our position by following God's instructions. We can take an active role in our deliverance and healing by changing our attitude, thinking, and perception of where we are. Jesus is the Healer and Deliverer of every situation! He can change the situation, or He can change us in the situation. Either way, a change takes place, and we are able to move from a place of hopelessness to hopefulness. Sin can shipwreck our lives; doubt and unbelief are silent killers. Hope in Christ and His ability is the only cure! Do not wait another day in a defeated position—rise up and walk!

*Faith hopes!*

## Hebrews 11:1

*Father, forgive me for the sin of unbelief, I acknowledge my sin, and I ask that You cleanse me and sanctify my heart today. I realize that I can do nothing without You, but with Christ I can do all things. I ask that You show me what You want me to do, and how You want me to do it. I choose to get up today by accepting Your healing and deliverance for what ails me! I choose to believe and rise up from this place of hopelessness! You, Lord, are my hope! In Jesus' Name, Amen.*

# Day 16

Read: *2 Corinthians 4:13*

"*I have believed, and therefore have I spoken.*"

## "Life Shapers"

It is so easy to speak about our problems and how we feel. It is natural to discuss how we are feeling to our family, friends, and anyone who will listen. Our conversations can at times be negative. God calls negative conversations idle words. Words that have no ability to produce life. God wants us to speak words of life, faith, and hope! Positive faith-based speech has the power to change our future. Negative words have life and will shape our future too. We must take control over our thoughts and the things that we say. We must find something positive to speak about, but first we must think thoughts that are positive. We can ask the Lord to help us control our thoughts and speech by making us become aware of what we say. We must gain control of our speaking and our thoughts. How we shape our lives will depend on what we think and what we say!

*God hears what we say.*

## Matthew 12:36

*Father, I often speak contrary to Your promises. I repent and ask for forgiveness for negative speech! Lord, cleanse my heart, my mind, and my speech today. Lord, help me to speak things that are filled with life. Lord, help me to set a watch over my own mouth. In Jesus' Name, Amen.*

# Day 17

Read: *Matthew 6:19–21*

*"For where your treasure is, there will your heart be also."*

## "Missed Fortune"

The lust for material wealth and more stuff runs rampant in our society. Obtaining more is always the pursuit, and when more is obtained, it is not enough. Lust is a part of the sinful nature, and we must master its dictates. Lust always wants, and there is no end. It is far wiser to put our desire and wants on things worth obtaining. Having the Lord in our corner, and on our side is the most blessed, prosperous and rich position we could attain. A close relationship with the Lord is a better investment than accumulating material novelties.

In pursuing real treasure, we have to store up time with the Lord, living for Him, and doing for Him, and giving to Him the treasure of our lives. We cannot give Him the best part of us chasing after the best parts of this world. He told us to pursue Him, and He would bless us with all other things. We do not want to miss our true fortune! We are to keep our eyes open, and not be blinded by the glamour of this world's goods. Cultivating an intimate and personal relationship with Him is key to successful godly living. Putting our faith, trust, and desire in the Lord will give us a better return on our investment than anything else!

*Trusted treasure!*

## Psalm 20:7

*Father, I have trusted in many things. I repent for getting off track and pursuing things that will not bring any eternal and lasting rewards. Help me to discipline my flesh and cut off the dictates of the flesh. I choose to live holy and acceptable to You, which is my reasonable service. I want to pursue Your kingdom, and I ask for Your help. In Jesus' Name, Amen.*

# Day 18

Read: *2 Kings 22:1-20*

*"And when the king heard the words of the Book of the Law, he rent his clothes."*

## "In the Midst"

Ungodliness and wickedness all around us is not a license for us to slack in our commitment to righteous, holy living. We can remain true to God and follow Him in times of corruption, apostasy, and violence. These times are not an excuse for riotous living by the believer. God will bring judgment upon such behavior, and He will cut off and destroy people and nations for such conduct. Those that would continue to live holy lives must stay tenderhearted, penitent, and humble before the Lord. We are to take the position of prayer, intercession, petition, and supplication for ourselves, people, and nations, even while the fate of evil conduct is certainly sealed!

Josiah repented and prayed! He was determined to follow God, make changes in the land that adhered to God's Word, destroy evil, wickedness, and idolatry. We are to remain committed to godly standards, take a righteous stand against ungodliness, and commit ourselves heart, soul, and mind to God and His precepts and principles! Godly sorrow for sin must forever be the position of our hearts; prayer for the repentance and salvation of people must be our active supplication. Conformity to God and His Word must be our daily conduct. God's Truth must forever be the standard we live by, no matter what the rest of the world may be doing around us.

*Remain steadfastly devoted to God!*

## Hosea 6:6

*Father, I repent for conforming to the world's pattern of living. I ask for forgiveness for my failure to put Your Word first! I rededicate myself to Your precepts and principles. Grant me strength to conform my life and my ways to Your counsel. Show me today where I need to make changes to my life to live holy and righteous before you. Let the standard of Your holiness be my compass. In Jesus' Name, Amen.*

*Day 19*

Read: *Matthew 27:27–44*

*"He is the King of Israel."*

## "Mission Accomplished"

God's love in me does not provoke me to choose the way of self-preservation. If we would just look at the crucifixion and how it took place, and what took place, we would see easily that it really didn't have to play out the way it did. Jesus was always in control, but when we look at his situation from a worldly perspective, it would appear Jesus had no choice. However, Jesus always had a choice; from the very beginning, Jesus had a choice. What is so awesome about what He did for mankind is the fact that He didn't have to do it. He chose to do it. That is love! It is also commitment. He loved us enough to come to earth to die for us. He also was committed to what He had been chosen to do.

I can't help but think about myself and all the things I think about giving up on. The things that I do not want to keep on doing, and the things I refuse to commit myself to doing. I think about what I want to quit, and what I should not have to put up with. I say to myself, "Why should I? I don't have to." The truth is, I don't have to, but when faced with my Savior's sacrifice, I recognize that I too have a choice to fulfill my Father's will, or my own. I realize my attitude has to change in light of the revelation that I do not have to do anything I do not want to do when it comes to living the Christian life. I do have a choice. I can follow my Savior's example of enduring the shame, mockery, scorn, and disrespect of people as I live and stand for Christ, or I can self-preserve by throwing in the towel on any and everything I just don't want to be bothered with anymore. In thinking about Jesus, I cannot in good conscience throw in the towel, not when He endured the cross for me. Somehow, some way, I must endure to the end too. I realize too that this decision is love, my love for Jesus.

*Pick up your cross and follow Me.*

## Matthew 16:24

*Father, forgive me for wanting to give up and throw in the towel on this life I have been given. You gave your life for me, help me to give my life for You. I want to be able to stand and endure circumstances rather than run and fold. Give me strength and the mind to stand, endure, and complete Your agenda. In Jesus' Name, Amen.*

# Day 20

Read: *Galatians 5:13–26*

*"For you, brethren, were (indeed) called to freedom."*

## "Crisis Control"

We are to manage our emotions even in times of difficulty and crisis. Our conduct is to be one of holiness and a reflection of the Gospel of Christ. We are not to allow our freedom in Christ, God's forgiveness, grace, and long-suffering to be an excuse to act ugly! God's grace is not our ticket to conduct ourselves according to the godless human nature. God's expectation for our behavior is to reflect His Word. Our manner of life matters to Him!

Self-control is a fruit of the Holy Spirit. It is one of the nine gifts of the Holy Spirit that the presence of God works in us, if we allow Him to do the work. The Holy Spirit must be at work in me to help me practice self-restraint, especially in a time of crisis and difficulty. If we allow the Holy Spirit to lead, guide and control us, He will work the fruit of self-control and self-restraint in us, and our conduct and behavior will be led by God's Spirit and not our own.

*Free to be like Christ*

## Philippians 1:27

*Father, thank You for Your Holy Spirit which works Christ's nature in me! I repent of acting, reacting, and responding with my own nature in times of crisis and difficulty. Help me to die daily to my own nature and put on the nature and character of Christ and His Spirit. I yield to Your ways and not my own. I thank You for Your help to be like Christ! In Jesus' Name, Amen.*

# Day 21

Read: *Psalm 91:15, 16*

*"He shall call upon Me."*

## "His Care"

God wants to help us, but we must allow Him to be our help. As humans we have the natural tendency to do for ourselves, to take care of ourselves. Our culture even stresses for us to "do things for ourselves." However, in the kingdom of God, we are taught by the Word of God to trust in the Lord instead. We are repeatedly directed to not lean and rely on self, but to trust and put our confidences in the Lord and what He is able to do for us. His power and His might are ever before us in the scriptures. We are reminded to put no trust in self or anyone else. In fact, Jeremiah 17:5 (NLT) says, *"Cursed are those who put their trust in mere humans, who rely on human strength and turn their hearts away from the LORD."* We are humans, and putting trust in ourselves brings a curse!

We must challenge ourselves daily to put our confidence and trust in the Lord. We must first humble ourselves before the Lord, then entrust Him with our concerns, fears, anxieties, and worries. This is a better way for us than trying to take care of ourselves and making a mess of our lives. God is faithful, and if we decide to make Him our trust and confidence, He will honor us with His care!

*God's way for self is demotion.*

## 1 Peter 5:6, 7

*Father, forgive me for self-confidence in myself. I ask You humbly for Your help and assistance with all of life's issues, problems, and circumstances. I repent for putting confidence and trust in anything other than You and depending on my own way. Realign my thinking and my attitude to lean on, rely on, and trust in Your abilities and not my own self-care. In Jesus' Name, Amen.*

# Day 22

Read: *Philippians 4:8, 9*

*"Think on and weigh and take account of these things (fix your minds on them)."*

## "Peaceful Results"

Our thought life is a major contributor to our day-to-day existence. Will we live in a positive, fulfilling, hopeful existence or in a negative, down-and-out, hopeless existence? The choice is totally up to us and whatever we allow to come into, and let rest in, our thoughts. Depression is a process. It is a spiraling downward into self-pity, hopelessness, and despair, and can even cause death through suicide. Depression is real and it yields real results of its presence. Depression can be caused by generational curses, life-debilitating circumstances, unfulfilled desires and pursuits, mental, physical, emotional, and spiritual exhaustion, an inability to move forward in life, sin, and many other causes. However, God gives us a prescription in His Word to overcome any trigger that is loaded with depression to take us on a journey downward.

No matter what we are faced with, go through, or are presently in, or the residue we carry from our past, we are to obtain, have, and develop a good report! This good report must be what is in, and on our minds. Our thoughts must be one of a good, positive, and true report. God's Word is the truth ... period, the end! God tells us that our thinking will produce actions, and our actions will produce what takes place in our day-to-day living. Will our days be negative, filled with anxiety, worry, fear, and fretfulness; or positive, filled with well-being, contentment, courage, and peace? The choice is ours and we must be wise in how we choose—our day depends on it!

*Positive thinking, Positive actions, yield Peaceful Results.*

## Philippians 4:9

*Father, help me to guard the gates of my mind today. Let my thoughts rest in a good report according to the council and truth of Your Word! I take ever thought captive and bring it into the obedience of Your Word. I repent of negative thinking, speaking, and doing. Cleanse me and wash my negative, faithless thought life! I choose to have a good, perfect, and positive word for my day today. In Jesus' Name, Amen.*

# Day 23

Read: *Romans 4:7, 8*

*"Blessed, and happy to be envied are those whose iniquities are forgiven."*

## "House Cleaning"

Forgiveness is not an option for those of us that have been forgiven by God. The person who has accepted Christ as their Personal Savior and has called on His Name to be saved from their sins must be a forgiving person… period! God has *"forgiven, covered up, and completely buried our sins"* (Romans 4:7 AMP). In light of that Truth, we ought not to keep a record of the wrongs done to us! This does not mean we are not to acknowledge when someone has done something wrong to us. There can be a genuine wrong done to us, or a perceived wrong. When either happens, we are not to hold the wrong against the person. This way, the wrong is not planted in our hearts and resentment doesn't turn into bitterness in us and yields a tree of unforgiveness. As godly offspring, we must love, and practice immediately ridding ourselves of the wrongs done to us. We have to get better and stronger in forgetting some things and cling less to the memories of hurt and offense.

Let's do some spiritual house cleaning TODAY! Those records on "memory lane" of wrongs done to you—stamp them "paid in full." Choose to give your thoughts to those things that will help you, encourage you, and lighten your heart. Those old records of wrongs towards you, forgive them, cover them up, and completely bury them. Like God did for us! God expects it!

*Choose your thoughts and memories based on love.*

# 1 Corinthians 13:5

*Father, I accept Your forgiveness, and I thank You for Your grace and mercy towards me. Forgive me, Lord, for holding a record of wrongs against anyone. I release them now in Jesus' Name. No one owes me anything! I Forgive today and choose to love instead. Help me to think upon good things that build up, encourage, and bring joy. I pray for blessing and comfort towards those that have genuinely wronged me, and for any wrongs that I have perceived. I declare and decree that forgiveness, love, grace and mercy live in me! In Jesus' Name, Amen.*

# Day 24

Read: *Proverbs 16:9*

*"But the Lord directs his steps and makes them sure."*

## "Secure Steps"

Life has a way of knocking us off course. We plan our days and our futures as we see in our own minds. However, God many times has another plan for us entirely. When we encounter the difficulty of having to re-evaluate and revamp our lives, we are met with instability, confusion, and indecisiveness. Our plans have been thwarted, and we must take a step back and begin to reflect on what is most important to God and not what is most important to us. When our steps become stagnant and we are unsure of our way, God is the person who can give our steps the right course and stabilize our way forward. He will cause His purposes and His plans for us to succeed, if we allow Him access to our plans.

God will make His plans for us secure because He is obligated to His purposes and His plans. His way for us is always the best way forward. We need his power, peace, and wisdom to be successful in the life He has given to us. We all want to be successful and feel a sense of accomplishment with our lives. God is the author and finisher of any success we can attain when we live our life securely in Him. We should be mindful to always give God the right to interfere with our plans, so that we stay in successful pursuit of a life that will please Him.

*Move on today in what God has planned for you.*

## Jeremiah 29:11

*Father, I thank You that You know all things, and all things consist of and have their being in You. You know the plans You have for me, and I desire to walk in the plans You have designed for my success. Grant me discernment to know the paths and directions You want me to take. Make my steps sure and secure in Your instructions. Forgive me any disobedience to Your will and Your way, and place my feet on the path of righteousness according to Your purposes and plans. In Jesus' Name, Amen.*

# Day 25

Read: *Ephesians 4:1–2*

*"Living as becomes you with complete lowliness of mind (humility)..."*

## "Make Allowances"

It takes humility (lowliness of mind) to make allowances and bear with the faults of others. We are all human and no one is perfect. We should not be the type of person that insists on our own way all the time. This type of behavior comes out of a personality that is selfish, self-centered, and lacking the God kind of love. We must develop and cultivate a heart and mind that allows for the weaknesses and faults of other people. We must also make allowances for our own mistakes and human frailties. God loves us no matter how many mistakes we make, and He loves us with all our imperfections. We have to not be so hard on ourselves, and we have to stop being so hard on other people. We all need allowances because we are all human.

Pride will keep us from being able to put up with other people's imperfections, including our own! Making allowances is love in action and a summons to God's service! God loves us and He surely makes allowances for us! We must love ourselves and we must love others, and we can demonstrate this love by making allowances and bearing with the human weaknesses of others.

*Allow for human error.*

# Romans 3:23

*Father, forgive me for being so hard on myself for mistakes I have made. I forgive myself today. Forgive me for being hard hearted and unyielding with others and their faults and weaknesses. You forgive me and my weaknesses, and today I make a decision to be a person that practices making allowances for others. Pour Your love in me today so that I have mercy and grace in me to meet the imperfections of others and the imperfections in myself. In Jesus' Name, Amen.*

# Day 26

Read: *Lamentations 3:24–26*

*"The Lord is good to those who wait hopefully and expectantly for Him."*

## "Key to Hope"

The things we suffer can cause us to develop a negative attitude about life. A hard life helps to shape our expectation. The enemy of our soul has a purpose in devastating our lives with abuse, hurt, pain, loss, and neglect. These are a few expectation shapers, but there can be many more that cause us to despair and suffer disappointment. We often end up with a negative attitude and outlook on life. "Nothing good" becomes our expectation, and this breeds an attitude of negativity. We must let go of the disappointment of our past and look forward to the hope of our future. We cannot move into our future with a negative attitude. Instead, we must move into our future with hope, faith, and trust in God. We must rid ourselves of the despair and disappointment of past circumstances. We must turn our negative thoughts and words into positive ones! We must develop the practice of being positive in every situation that arises.

We must come to realize that our lives cannot change until our attitude takes on a new level of faith. We must begin to hope no matter what is happening, good or bad circumstances. Our hope, faith, and trust must be placed in the Lord! We must develop a discipline to maintain a positive attitude toward life. We must feed our hope with positivity, and wait for our awesome God to fulfill His plans for our lives. A key to hope is developing, maintaining, and rehearsing a positive attitude. Draw a healthy positive attitude from God's Word. God is positive and He wants to satisfy us with good things, when we hope for them.

*Put your hope in God every day!*

## Psalm 39:7

*Father, I turn to You today in hope, faith, and trust! I look to You and believe You love me and will work the circumstances in my life for Your good and glory. Help me to wait expectantly for You to move on my behalf and to maintain a good attitude of faith, hope, and trust. In Jesus' Name, Amen.*

# Day 27

Read: *Proverbs 9:10-11*

*"The reverent and worshipful fear of the Lord is the beginning (the chief and choice part) of Wisdom."*

## "Wisdom is Greater"

God has given mankind a great gift. He has given man a mind. We have a mind to think, reason, and make decisions, choices, and determinations based on knowledge—what we know. We utilize God's gift to develop our lives, to pursue dreams, and cultivate our relationships. God has given us an ability to obtain knowledge by using our mind and its ability to think. However, there is a better gift than knowledge. There is wisdom. Wisdom that comes from God and is not dependent on knowledge alone.

Living dependent on what we know can hinder us from trusting God and His promises to us. Trust in God requires us to believe God when we don't necessarily see how things can work out based on what we know. Trust requires us to depend on God and His promises rather than the facts that are presented to us. There will be situations in life where faith in God and the power of His Word are better than depending on the knowledge we think we possess. We will have to put reason aside, our knowledge under the promises of God's Word, and trust God beyond what we know. Wisdom is better than knowledge when we need God to do a miracle above and beyond our knowledge.

*Wisdom is better.*

## Proverbs 8:11

*Father, I desire to trust in You and Your promises rather than reason by my own thinking and knowledge. Forgive me for trusting in myself and my own thinking rather than trusting in Your ability to work in my life for Your own glory. I repent for reasoning and ask that You help me to trust in Your ability, and not my own. I take hold of your promises today and believe in Your Word. Divine Wisdom comes from You, and it is far better to trust in Your Wisdom than in my own knowledge. In Jesus' Name, Amen.*

# Day 28

Read: *Psalm 91*

*"Only a spectator shall you be (yourself inaccessible in the secret place of the Most High) as you witness the reward of the wicked."*

## "Covert Operation"

Fighting the good fight of faith has an outfit that does not always require us to get in the dirt and mix it up with demons, spiritual wickedness, principalities, and powers in high places. "Rest" is a garment we can wear for war! *"The Shadow of the Almighty (Whose power no foe can withstand)"* is able to cover and protect us. We can remain in His Shadow and fight some battles from "the secret place" of REST! The Lord is able to protect me in this place, and He fights the battle for me.

There will be times that we will find ourselves in the trenches where spiritual warfare will require a covert operation tactic, "an operation that is so planned and executed as to conceal the identity of or permit plausible denial by the sponsor. Covert operations aim to secretly fulfill their mission objective without any parties knowing who sponsored or carried out the operation." (Wikipedia by North America 1000). The Almighty fights for us as we stand in faith, trusting in His ability to defend us in situations that are beyond what we can handle. *"His strength is made perfect in our weakness."* We can rest in the Almighty's Presence, and watch from a place of faith, safety, and protection, God's operation against the enemy on our behalf!

*Fight in God's ability!*

## 1 Corinthians 12:9

*Father, You are Almighty, and nothing can win against You! I submit to your authority and Your protection. I trust in Your ability to protect me, and I confidently put my trust in You! Lord, help me to fight the good fight of faith! Evil may be all around me, but I trust that You, Almighty God, are my defense! In Jesus' Name, Amen.*

# Day 29

Read: *Leviticus 11:1-12, 41-45*

*"You shall be holy, for I am holy."*

## "Visible Devotion"

In Leviticus, God is instructing the Israelites on what they can and cannot eat. It appears that God has an interest in the eating habits of His people. One might view the passage as a tip on healthy eating choices. However, in looking at one deeper meaning to this passage, health may be just a by-product of a more significant theme. These instructions followed by God's chosen people would be a visible sign to other nations of their obedience to their God. Their actions through their obedience would make them distinct from other nations.

There are things that are supposed to make us as Christians distinct from the world and its systems. As Christians, we are commanded by our God *"to be holy as He is holy."* Food laws are not used any longer as a distinctive mark for the people of God. (Mark 7:14–23, Acts 10:9–15). However, we should definitely have behaviors that make us visibly distinguishable as God's people! We are to be holy! In other words, we are to be entirely devoted to our God! We are to be consecrated and set apart for God's use and God's purposes. Our lives are to be a reflection of Him and all that He is, and He says He is holy. Holiness can be seen. What are we looking like to the world?

*Be holy like the One who called you.*

## 1 Peter 1:16

*Father, You have commanded that I be holy. Holiness apart from You is futile! So, I ask that You sanctify my life daily by Your Word and by Your Spirit. Give me a willing heart, mind, and body to submit to You and Your ways. Help me to be dedicated and entirely devoted to You. Lord, help me to see where there are idols in my life and empower me to tear them down. You be first in my life! Let my life show that Jesus is Lord! In Jesus' Name, Amen.*

# Day 30

Read: *2 Corinthians 4:8–18*

*"So we look not at the things which are seen, but at the things which are unseen."*

## "See Your Way Out"

Our inner man is renewed day by day through God's grace. Though the outward part of us is perishing, we do not have to be discouraged by this because God's grace is available for our renewal every day. Though we may be experiencing trials and afflictions, this is good because without them we cannot experience the graces of our God. His grace is manifold because there are many graces, and His graces are multidimensional in our lives. We are blessed on every side and in every way despite what we are experiencing. While we cannot earn these graces, they abound toward us because of God's great love towards us. God's graces are working for us in every way in the here and now, and they are preparing for our future blessedness in eternity.

Be thankful that God's graces are always working for us, not against us. Be comforted in knowing that what we are seeing and experiencing in this life is not the final outcome of our existence, but the working of bigger, better, and the best of what God's graces have planned for our blessed eternity. Rest assured that God's graces are always working.

*Faith sees a bright future.*

## Hebrews 12:2

*Father, thank You for my life today, every part of it. I recognize that in my difficult circumstances, I have the opportunity to experience the many facets of your graces and mercies. I acknowledge your multifaceted graces operating in my life right now. Lord, I say thank You today for grace working in my life now, and grace working for my life in eternity. In Jesus' Name, Amen.*

# Day 31

Read: *Psalm 37:3*

*"Trust (lean on, rely on, and be confident) in the Lord and do good."*

## "People Matter"

Trusting God is a goal we as believers strive to do daily. We desire to put our trust, confidence, and hope in the Lord. We want to please God by having faith in Him. The scripture tells us that *"without faith it is impossible to please God."* Scripture also says, *"Cast not away your confidence"* (Hebrews 10:35). We know that without believing, trusting, and putting our faith, hope, and confidence in God, we cannot expect to get anything from Him. However, we are to also do good. Having faith and confidence in God is His expectation, but doing good towards others is also His expectation. Loving others from a pure heart is what is important to God. God has always cared about people!

Let no one deceive you into believing that God's priority is not people. God's goal is to win the hearts of people with and through the love of His Son, Jesus. Jesus died so that we could be won! That is the love of Christ! The Father and the Son were both motivated by love for people. What motivates us? We should be motivated by love from a pure heart. We should have no hidden agendas or motives when it comes to doing good towards people. Have faith, yes, but remember there is another part to faith—to do good.

*Be motivated by love.*

# 1 Timothy 1:5

*Father, help me to change my attitude. Love is important to You and therefore, should be what is important to me. Forgive me for not doing good to people, who You have created and who You are concerned for. It is my desire to believe You, to trust You, and be confident in You. Today let me take on another important direction from You. Teach me how to do good. In Jesus' Name, Amen.*

# Day 32

Read: *Esther 4:5–16*

*"Then I will go to the king, though it is against the law and if I perish, I perish."*

## "God First"

God has called each one of us *"for such a time as this."* We are not a mistake or mishap! God knows right where we are and has not lost sight of us! The enemy of our souls wants us to accept the lie that God has forgotten us, but God has a plan for the life of each one of us. Right where we are God can use us for his glory and honor! Esther had been taken captive against her will and that seemed such a horrible fate to endure, but God had a plan and a purpose for her, and for the lives of His people. What God calls us to is never just about us, but about the lives of the people we are to touch. Our job is to keep God first and place Him above everything, so that He can get the glory from our lives, and so that we can be pleasing to Him. This is the wisdom we as kingdom-minded people of God are to *strive* for. Proverbs 9:10 says, *"The reverent and worshipful fear of the Lord is the beginning (the chief and choicest part) of Wisdom and the knowledge of the Holy One is insight and understanding."*

The world would have us concentrate on what we can do for ourselves and on seeking our own agendas and plans. John 15:6 tells us that apart from God we can do nothing! God wants to use us in ways that we could never seek out for ourselves. He wants us to be successful and fruitful but not outside of Him. I am sure Esther had no idea that she would be used to save a nation! But at the end of the day, Esther had to choose to put God and His agenda before the comfort and pleasure of her own life. We see that Esther did choose to handle God's business and agenda, and a nation of people were saved because of her decision to serve God First!

*God gives us the power to be bold.*

## Acts 4:33

*Father, give to me boldness and courage to do the things You ask of me. Help me to accomplish Your will and not be centered on my own desires and pursuits. It is You that I desire to please and ask that by Your Holy Spirit, You grant me power to complete those things You put before me. In Jesus' Name, Amen.*

# Day 33

Read: *Philippians 3:9, 10*

*"For my determined purpose is that I may know Him."*

## "His Terms"

A healthy, right relationship with God is based on His terms, not our own. It is all about what God wants, needs, and expects, not what we want, what we need, and what we expect. Obtaining this mind and heart and purpose is the reverential fear of the Lord. Now how do we get there when we are so far off that mark? How do we cultivate a relationship on God's terms and not our own? How do we accept His terms? We begin through genuine faith in Jesus Christ. We must pursue a lifestyle of righteousness motivated by faith and not a righteousness based on obedience to the Law through ritualistic duties. Self-achieved righteousness carries out the demands of God's Law. A relationship with God through faith believes God and pursues an intimate relationship with Him. The goal becomes to know God better, to understand Him more deeply, and to seek His heart and His mind's desire more consistently.

The prize in a relationship based on God's terms is always God Himself. When we lose sight of the true reward of an intimate relationship with God, we have lost our focus. Regain the right perspective today and reunite with God on His terms.

*God rewards the seeker.*

## Hebrews 11:6

*Father, I desire to have a relationship based on Your terms. Forgive me for doing things my way and expecting You to bend to my will. I am sorry! I want a relationship with You based on Your terms. Teach me Your way, God. Lord, help me to not lose sight of my true reward as your disciple. You are my reward! In Jesus' Name, Amen.*

# Day 34

Read: *Luke 5:12-16*

*"And Jesus reached out His hand and touched him, saying, 'I am willing.'"*

## "The Untouchables"

This leper had the courage to seek Jesus out. He came to Jesus as he was, seeking help from someone he believed could help him. This man was an "untouchable." Jesus, however, touches him! We can learn from this passage that God is willing to touch the untouchable—Jesus says so, he says to this leper, "I am willing." Christ is willing to touch the diseased, the chronically sick, the hopeless, the terminally ill, the infectious, and the incurable. There can be risks in touching the lives of people, but Christ took those risks to bring healing, health, and wholeness to the untouchables of this world. People are looking for hope, looking for help, looking for someone to care enough, love enough, and have enough compassion to "be willing" to touch them in their incurable state.

If we be in Christ, and His Spirit lives in us, we should be, would be, and will be willing to touch those that need the healing hand of Christ. Jesus was willing—are you?

*Let compassion move you!*

## Ephesians 4:32

*Father, fill me with Your Spirit to enable me to bring the healing deliverance, compassion, and love of Christ to those who are looking for hope and health for their issues. Christ is the power of God, and His blood was shed for me and all that would believe in Him. Lord, You have touched my life; let me be willing to touch others. Let this same mind of Christ be in me. In Jesus' Name, Amen.*

# Day 35

Read: *Genesis 13:9–18*

*"Then Lot chose for himself."*

## "Choose to Look Up"

There are many choices in life for us to decide upon. Discernment is a needed gift to help us navigate through our spiritual walk. The Holy Spirit is always to be our guide, but even with His help, we can be at a crossroad wondering if we are following God's best for us in our choices. The good will always be an enemy to God's best for our life. Our right to choose becomes the guiding factor for our lives, and it is crucial that we obtain godly, spiritual insight when making decisions.

We see in this passage Lot choosing what he thought was the best of the land for himself. Lot, Abram's nephew, left Ur along with Abram. I don't see where he was invited, but he left with Abram nevertheless. Here Lot considers Abram, and thinks about himself first, and chooses the best land. Lot's choice was based on appearance and what looked better for himself (v.11). Looks can be deceiving! What looks good is not always the best or better choice! Lot's choice led him to dwell in Sodom, and we know how that ended. God did not give Lot the land He chose nor bless the land he chose.

Abram, on the other hand, yielded his right to choose what was best for himself by giving Lot first choice of the land. Abram accepted what appeared to be what was left of the lands. Land that did not look as good as the land Lot chose. God, however, reveals here, that He can bless us wherever we are when we yield our right to choose what is best for ourselves. When we trust Him to work things for our good on the soil of the places where we think we just ended up. God can bless us in places that do not look as blessed and prosperous as some other people's lives we see "over there." God told Abram to *"lift up his eyes and look from the place where you are."* God gave Abram the land he was in, and he blessed the land he was in. Choosing God's will does not mean we will look like we are blessed because of what we gain, but that we will be blessed in what we already have, and where we are. God's blessing and God's increase makes the difference in His children's prosperity.

*Yield your right to choose.*

## Psalm 25:4, 5, 10

*Father, I choose this day to walk in Your path for me, not the path of my own desires. I choose the life You have planned for me. I know I mess up and make my own plans for just about everything. I repent and ask for forgiveness for my knowing and unknowing disobedience. Lord, I ask that this insensitive leading of my own heart and way would cease! Lord, show me Your way; I want to follow. Holy Spirit, help me follow the Father for all my decisions and choices. In Jesus' Name, Amen.*

# Day 36

Read: *Romans 8:16–18*

*"The glory that is about to be revealed later to us and in us and for us and conferred on us!"*

## "No Comparison"

God reveals Himself to us in our suffering. If we will be still and listen for His voice, He will speak to us, and reveal His direction, guidance, correction, and instructions. God through His Holy Spirit is our help in times of distress, hardship, trials, and yes, even temptations. God reveals His glory in us as we go through our own personalized suffering. As His children, He is shaping us individually into the image of His Son. God has promised to work all things for our good. In allowing this Truth to settle in us, we must obey God in the suffering, knowing He is working on our behalf. The nature of our suffering Savior is developed in us, and the glory of God is revealed through us. God anoints us with His power, authority, and endurance to go through difficulty. When we want nothing more than to run out of these hard places, God through His Holy Spirit empowers us to go through them instead, and obtain the victory of overcoming. God sustaining us in our suffering is His glory conferred on us.

Nothing can compare with the reward God has in store for those who suffer and endure hardship as a good soldier. As His children, let us continue to walk in obedience to His will, no matter what it looks like and no matter what we go through. God will do great things in our lives as we continue to move forward in faith, trusting Him to be our way out.

*Allow Him to help.*

## Psalms 124:8

*Father, suffering never seems pleasant, but I pray today that as I grow and mature, I will obtain the power to overcome suffering and go through to victory rather than allow suffering to render me helpless. I pray that I will be strong in the Lord, and in the power of His might! I pray that Your Glory will be my focus! In Jesus' Name, Amen.*

# Day 37

Read: *2 Corinthians 4:6, 7*

*"However, we possess this precious treasure."*

## "Hearing Light"

As offspring of God, we need to be able to hear His voice. Hearing God requires spending time in His Word. We are to listen for His Truth and grab hold of it for comfort, guidance, and growth. When someone speaks to us a word of wisdom and knowledge, we are to listen for God's Truth in those words. When there is no connection with God and His Word, from the words we hear, those words are not from the wisdom that comes from God. Worldly wisdom is not from above and does not come from God's Truth.

Hearing God also requires us to take time in God's Presence to learn how to reach within to hear His voice. When listening through our heart, there must be the precious treasure of God's divine light of life and power living on the inside of us. From within, His voice of Truth gives us wisdom, knowledge, understanding, and direction for our lives. Hearing God requires time in His Word, and time in His Presence. We must take the time to learn how to listen.

*Hearing takes time to listen.*

## Romans 10:17

*Father, thank You for the Truth that comes from Your Word. Teach me to hear You from a place of Truth. Train my ear and my heart to listen for the Truth that is Your Word. Let my life, and the direction I walk, be lit with the Truth of the Gospel. Holy Spirit, lead me daily to take time to hear and listen to the Truth that is found in the Word of God. In Jesus' Name, Amen.*

# Day 38

Read: *Psalm 119:165*

*"Great peace have they who love your law."*

## "Mind Peace"

The Peace of God is needed to keep our minds healthy and whole. We cannot function effectively in life with a mind that is in turmoil, confusion, and torment. Today we have so many contributors to mental illness. Our minds are delicate and intricate, and healing for our minds can be hit and miss depending on the doctor, the medicine, and the counseling. Who can heal the mind and make it completely whole? God can! God has created us in in His image, after His likeness. He is the creator of everything, including our mind. He knows exactly how our mind ought to function.

The beginning of a sound mind starts with loving God's law. While some people may need medicine and therapy, this does not negate the fact that we need God to help us in our daily walk in healing. God's law is a stabilizer, it's our shield, it's our strength to enable us in our healing and pursuit of daily wholeness. God's law is the doorway to peace. The scripture says, *"Great peace."* This is not a little bit of peace; this indicates a whole lot of peace. When the mind is troubled and sick, great peace is a blessing! Taking hold of the Word of God is a first step in entering God's peace. Learning to love God's Word is how we stay in the Peace of God.

*Receiving it, loving it, obeying it*

## Psalm 119:5

*Father, thank You for Your Peace. I pray today for Peace to garrison my mind and heart. I purpose myself to follow Your Peace found in the Word of God. Give me a heart and mind that delights in pursuing Your Peace. I put Your Word first in my life, and I lean on and rely on the benefits that your law affords me. In Jesus' Name, Amen.*

# Day 39

Read: *Psalm 145:13–21*

*"The Lord upholds ..."*

## "More Hope"

When we experience times of bitter hardship, our trust and confidence in the Lord is challenged. We can begin to not trust in God and His Word, because we do not understand the affliction we are going through. Bitter pills of life can make us spiritually sick! We only have to look at the story of Naomi in the Bible to gain the facts that loss, affliction, and grief affect our heart and our hope. Misfortune, especially when it comes in waves, brings discouragement, but our God is the God of Hope, and He is able to administer to us more hope!

God is able to help us in our circumstances, no matter what it is we are facing. God is able to sustain us! He is able to raise us up and renew our life. God fulfills His promises—that is Truth! He does not always bring us through the way we want, or how we want the outcome to be, but bring us through He will! God is faithful to His promises! If we are weak, He can strengthen us, hold us up, and raise us up! He said so!

*We have a defender and ally!*

## Psalm 54:4

*Father, I come asking for help. I acknowledge that You are God and Lord over everything, even my circumstances! I ask for Your Strength and Power to sustain me and uphold me in my place of testing, trial, and/or affliction. You are the God of Hope, and You are able to measure out more hope to help me endure, come through, and overcome! I thank You, Father, that I am coming up and out in victory! In Jesus' Name, Amen.*

# Day 40

Read: *Matthew 13:1–17*

*"He who has ears (to hear), let him hear and heed My words."*

## "Right Response"

In the parables, there are hidden truths. These truths were made known to the disciples but were not made known to the others that were listening. As Christ's disciples, we are privileged to know the secrets of the kingdom. While we are in this world, we are taught to be separate from the world. We are to live a life that reflects the Christ we say we serve. The kingdom of heaven is a way of life for us who are children of the kingdom. The kingdom's systems, principles, and laws are what we are to govern our lives by. There is an expected harvest for the seed of God's Word in the lives of His offspring. During this season of His Word being planted in the earth, we as his disciples are to have an ear that hears, receives, and understands His teachings. Because we have heard, and we understand, we are to produce the fruit of right living, along with doing work that reflect a righteous life.

The Lord will return for the harvest of our lives, and we need to be wise in our hearing so that we can do all that is required to shine as children of the kingdom of heaven. We need to have a right response to the things we have heard!

*Hear and heed!*

## JAMES 1:22

*Father, make me to hear and heed Your Word. Open my ears and my eyes to hear and see Truth. Allow my heart to welcome the instructions from Your Word and to do what it commands. I ask that I be a doer of the Word and not just a hearer. Forgive me for ignoring Your Word and doing as I please. I ask for a changed heart and mind to obey the Word that I hear and to bear fruit that exemplifies a righteous life according the Word. In Jesus' Name, Amen.*

# Day 41

Read: *Matthew 21:12–22*

*"Do not doubt or allow yourself to be drawn in two directions."*

## "Particular Purpose"

There is so much to gain from this passage of scripture. We see the cleansing of the temple where Jesus drives out the money changers who were making a profit exchanging foreign money, and the selling of doves for sacrifice. Then later we see Jesus cursing a fig tree because he was hungry, but there was no fruit on the tree as he approached. We see two different events here, but there is a profound similarity in both. What we can glean from these two separate but similar events are Jesus' opposition to the use of things outside of what God has designed them to be. The temple was made for prayer; the fig tree was made to bear fruit.

We too have been designed by God for a particular purpose. We should ask ourselves today, are we being what God has designed us to be, and are we bearing fruit from the purpose that God has ordained? Today, let us reflect with wisdom what we are pursuing and doing with our life. We must put our lives on track with God's purpose and design for us. It is crucial to our success and to the blessing of God for a godly purpose, versus being cursed for self-interest and gain and a fruitless existence. Desire to move forward today in the right direction of fulfilling God's purpose.

*He made all things.*

# JOHN 1:3

*Father, I reflect today on my life, and what I am pursuing and doing. I repent for living for self and for what I think I can gain for myself. I pray for a refocus today on godly being and doing. Help me, Holy Spirit, to align my life with godly purpose and design. I know I will be blessed for bearing the fruit from Your original purpose for me. Lord, help me to go in the right direction. In Jesus' Name, Amen.*

# Day 42

Read: *Exodus 16:16–21*

*"This is what the LORD has commanded: Let every man gather as much of it as he needs."*

## "Daily Dependence"

What stands out in this portion of scripture is that the people had to depend on God to provide food for them to eat on a day-by-day basis. They were sustained by God's manna, and He provided for them what they needed to live on each day. God was teaching His people daily dependence upon Him. When the Israelites tried to prepare and feed themselves by trying to gather extra, the manna rotted. God gave specific instructions regarding the manna, and as long as they obeyed these instructions, they were fed by God Himself. God deliberately only provided what was needed for each day. The Israelites had to depend on Him each day to eat and live.

God wants to provide for us on a day-by-day basis today. He has given us specific instructions in His Word on how we should live a life that is pleasing, holy, and purposeful according to His kingdom's principles. All His instructions point out that He is to be our number one priority and that we are to follow these instructions if we want to live for Him and with Him. Eternity with Him is our permanent home and God wants us there! Like the Israelites and the manna, we must depend, trust, and obey God's instructions daily. God's instructions through His Word will protect, lead, guide, and sustain us in this life. Doing our own thing will ultimately result in rottenness.

*Daily trust and obey.*

## Proverbs 3:5, 6

*Father, thank You for providing for me every day. Lord, help me to trust and obey your instructions on godly living and holiness. I want to be led by Your Spirit and lead a life that is pleasing and honorable to You. Forgive me for not putting Your Word first in my life. I repent, ask for Your forgiveness, and turn to You for guidance and instruction for a holy consecrated life in You. In Jesus' Name, Amen.*

# Day 43

Read: *Psalm 62:6–8*

*"The Lord is my rock ..."*

## "The Rock"

While riding past my old neighborhood, my eyes focused on the playground where I spent many summer days. I noticed still standing was the set of swings that I swung so high on. That swing set was still standing after forty years! I thought to myself, those swings were put in on a strong foundation to be able to stand for such a long period of time. The swings were rusted and the bright pretty paint was gone, but the swing itself was still standing! The solid ground in that playground enabled the swings to endure through time.

David says in Psalms that the Lord is his rock and unyielding strength. A life built upon the Lord has the ability to last and endure through time. Winds may blow, rain may pour down, storm after storm may rise, but the one whose foundation is built upon the Rock, has a solid foundation. This foundation will give us the ability to endure life's challenges and go through them without going under. We are able to rise above the storms, weather the rain, and stand against the winds of adversity. If we make the Lord our rock, and firm foundation, we will be able to stand, and endure through time like a good old swing set!

*Stand Firm!*

## Proverbs 10:25

*Lord, I thank You for keeping me. I acknowledge Your supportive hand upon me and the security of Your Protection on my life. You enable me to stand firm and I thank You for Christ! He is my solid rock and sure foundation! In Jesus Name, Amen*

# Day 44

Read: *1 Kings 12*

*"For this thing has come about from me."*

## "The Controller"

Rehoboam followed advice from his peers, resulting in a nation of people rebelling and the kingdom being split. Division was the result of Rehoboam's decision to continue the forced labor of the people. Jeroboam's fear resulted in him leading the very people who chose him to be king, into idolatry and sin. We see here two kings whose rule over the people brought about results that were not good. However, we also see here that even though things went bad, God was still in control.

Our lives may at times seem out of control, it may feel that we have ended up in a place that we did not choose just because we may have made the wrong decision. We make choices and decisions expecting results to go in our favor, but that is not always the case. There will be many times that our choices will cause a ripple effect of a downward spiral. In those times, we must remember that God is still in control. We must look to take our direction from God on how we are to live with the outcome of our choices. Today, pray and ask God to give you direction on how He would have you move forward with life despite the situation that has not gone the way you intended. Remember, God is there, even in the midst of our messes.

*God is still in control!*

# Romans 8:28

*Father, I repent for some of the decisions and choices I have made. I many times take matters into my own hands and do wrong, knowingly and sometimes unknowingly. I ask for forgiveness for the rebellion and disobedience of my decisions and choices. I ask You today to help me move forward in life, living in the paths that You have chosen for me, taking responsibility for my own actions. I do not want to stay stuck in regret, but move on to victory and success despite the negative outcomes of my own decisions. In Jesus' Name, Amen.*

# Day 45

Read: *Psalm 149:1–9*

*"Praise the Lord!"*

## "Right Praise"

Here in this Psalm, the people of Israel are commanded to praise the Lord. So often we look for things to be going well, for happy times, and for good things to be happening for us to praise and worship the Lord. While we want to give God praise for the things He has done for us, and the many blessings He has given to us, that is not the encouragement to praise Him that we see here in this particular Psalm. He tells the Israelites to *"rejoice in their Maker, rejoice in their King, and to praise His Name with dancing."* The praise, the worship, the rejoicing, the celebration, and the dancing is in the King! The celebration is all about the Lord! Our noise of praise and worship, and yes, it is vocal and physical, is to be rooted in the Lord! It is God Himself that we are dancing, leaping, and shouting about. When this is the source of our praise and worship, we are able to praise Him no matter what is going on in our lives. We are able to maintain a lifestyle of worship, no matter whether things are good or not so good. The right praise and worship are centered in the Lord, but it also has the ability to make war in the spirit realm and do some damage to the enemy too! We can honor God by giving Him the praise that is due Him, and executing warfare in the spirit against our enemies! We have the two-edged sword of praise and worship!

*Center Praise and Worship!*

## Psalm 34:3

*Father, so often I am praising You and worshipping You for the things You are doing or the things You have done for me. I know that this is good and it's right, but Lord, I want an even deeper relationship with You that magnifies You and You alone! Holy Spirit, help me to be mindful to praise and worship God alone for who He is! Stabilize my life in the right praise, worship, and warfare! In Jesus' Name, Amen.*

# Day 46

Read: *Numbers 13:25–33*

*"Let us go up at once and take possession of it."*

## "Take Action"

Here in this passage of scripture, the Israelites are still in the desert. However, this was not God's plan for His people. He brought them out of Egypt to take them into a blessed place to call home. God's promise was to give them land. The spies were sent to assess the land, to prepare them to take possession of the land. Instead, they came back off course and out of focus from the original plan. God tells Moses in *Numbers 13:2*, *"I am going to give"* the land. Nowhere did He say see if you can take the land first. The mission to spy out the land went off course based on what they saw with their natural eyes. The promise of God was derailed because the spies lost sight of the purpose of the spying. Instead of focusing on what God promised, they looked at who they were as men, in light of the men they saw. Their own perception of themselves cost them entering into the promise of God in that season. They saw themselves small and insignificant in the sight of the giants that lived in the land. They lost sight of the fact that God promised them the land, and that God was with them to enable them to take the land.

We must remember that without God, we are nothing and we can do nothing! However, we are not to keep our eyes focused on who we are, but on who our God is. Caleb was a man of faith who said, *"We need to go up right now and take the land."* Caleb's focus was on what God said, not what he saw. God wants us to realize our future is what He says. We are to listen to what God says, take Him at His Word, and watch Him fulfill His promises to us. The formula for our success is to keep what God has promised us and told us to do in the forefront. We are not to look at the situation and make the decision to not move based on what we see, what we can or cannot do. God enables us to do the impossible! We are to *"go up at once and take possession"* of those things God has given us instructions to take! Do not lose sight of the instruction to take action. Do it!

*Go, I am giving you victory!*

# Deuteronomy 31:8

*Father, forgive me for not following through with Your instructions for my life. I repent of disobedience and a negative report to myself. Help me, Holy Spirit, to hear the instructions. Lord, let me not be governed by what I see, but to move in the direction of the instructions to fully obey and do what You have led me to do. I ask for courage, boldness, and the ability to act in faith to fulfill Your will for me. In Jesus' Name, Amen.*

# Day 47

Read: *Matthew 26:38–39*

*"Yet not as I will, but as You will."*

## "Aim to Please"

Obedience and the life of Christ for believers is to live to please the Father. Christ living in us is our hope of living an obedient life to God and His will. We must remember our desire will always be in conflict with His will for us. The struggle to obey, yield, comply, submit, and follow will always be there within us. Our desire must link up with God's will. We have to continually look at and assess our desires. We must examine our heart against the Word of God to sift out any areas of conflict to God's perfect will for us and make that place a Gethsemane for our own will. The successful Christian life is not a life lived for self, but one of sacrifice and obedience. We must daily reflect and ask God, "Are there any areas where I am imposing my will in this season?" If we find anything in conflict with His will for us, we are to destroy that thing. God's will must take precedence! Our pursuit as believers is to fulfill His will. Daily, our will must die, and the life of Christ in us must be aimed at pleasing Him!

*Always do what pleases Him*

## John 8:29

*Father, reveal to me any areas of my life that are out of Your will for me. I repent for forcing my own desires in order to gain happiness. It is You and Your will that I must follow to please You and be acceptable to You. I want to live my life as a true believer. Show your paths for me to live a victorious life in Christ Jesus to please You! In Jesus' Name, Amen.*

# Day 48

Read: *2 Kings 4:1-7*

*"So, she left him and shut the door behind her and her sons."*

## "Miracle of More"

The thing that sticks out to me in this passage is that the woman took Elisha at his word. She did what Elisha told her to do, regardless of the impossibility of what he was actually asking her to do—go borrow containers from your neighbors and pour the oil you have in the house into them. Now, you and I know that she did not have enough oil in that one little pot to fill a bunch of containers. Right away, my mind went to that fact. Had it been me, I would have gotten stuck right there! I'd have waited a minute, and then I would have reasoned within myself that I didn't have enough oil to fill no bunch of pots! That is what the natural mind does when God wants to perform a miracle. We get stuck at the instruction! The miracle God wants to do, never manifests because we cannot wrap our minds around how a thing can be done!

It takes faith and obedience to fulfill God's instructions. What God tells us to do to supply us with more than enough will take faith and courage to obey. The reasoning of the natural mind cannot take part in the miracle-working plan of God! We must move out in faith and do what He instructs. God is still working miracles today, and the same kind of faith the woman needed to provide for her and her sons is the faith we will need in order to experience the miracle-working power of God! If we want to see the miracle of more than enough in our lives, we have to follow the instructions!

*Now faith yields the impossible!*

## Hebrews 11:1

*Father, I need Now Faith to walk in this next season of life. I repent and ask for forgiveness for doubt, unbelief, and reasoning. Give me discernment when I begin to reason with the miracles you want to perform in my life. Miracles for my benefit and for Your Glory! I want to follow Your instructions and be obedient to You. I need Your help, and I invite you into my life to provide for me, protect me, and sustain me. Help me to really live in faith and obedience. In Jesus' Name, Amen.*

# Day 49

Read: *Judges 4:4–5*

*"Now Deborah, a prophetess, the wife of Lappidoth, was judging Israel at that time."*

## "Employed by God"

God is able to use us right where we are, if we allow him access to our lives. Deborah was a wife, a judge, and prophetess over Israel. She was a spokesperson for God and settled disputes among the people. We too are to be employed by God. We can represent Christ by first living according to His Word in the midst of family, friends, neighbors, and coworkers. How we live for the Lord is crucial to our witness and testimony as Christians. Secondly, we can be used by God no matter where we are to help other people.

We get no excuse to sit down on God and do nothing! God wants us active in serving Him and executing the gifts, talents, and skills He has given to us. Like Deborah, we have a life that we have been given for God to use to help others. God is about using people to serve people. We all have an assignment, and that assignment is not far off over the rainbow. So often, we are looking for a way to be relevant somewhere other than where we are. If God sees fit to send us somewhere else, that's great, but until He does, the assignment He gives us is where we live at right now! We must get busy doing what we have been born to do! Other people's lives depend on us living for God right where we are.

*Employ your gift!*

## 1 Peter 4:10

*Father, thank You for the life You have given me. I recognize that You have made me for Your glory and Honor. Lead me to the paths that employ my gifts and talents to serve You and humanity. I ask for Your guidance, power, and strength to fulfill Your will. I start today, and I start where I am to bring You glory! To God be all the glory, honor, and praise! In Jesus' Name, Amen.*

# Day 50

Read: *Hebrews 4:4–11*

*"Let us therefore make every effort to enter that rest."*

## "Access to Rest"

We enter the Lord's place of rest for us through the door of faith. Life can be such a struggle, especially for the believer who is trying to live according to God's Word. We struggle to do the right things; we try to keep watch over what we say. We make efforts to get along with our brothers and sisters in Christ. We try diligently to follow the Word of God, only to fail and come short. These are just a few of the things we as Christians struggle with. This does not include the struggles of life, our jobs and all the issues that arise out of work and career. The challenges of relationships such as spouse, family, and children. The maintenance of our physical bodies and our health. All these areas of life present their own struggles. God knew we would need a place of rest to cease from struggling in all these areas that shipwreck our faith. Shipwrecked faith produces disobedience. Where there is unbelief, disobedience is sure to follow. Disobedience results in rebellion against God, and now we are in a struggle with God too. We make our way hard by not believing God and so block our entrance into the rest of God.

God's Word is made active in our lives by our faith. We have to believe God and cease from our effort to do right. Our human effort to live will not produce rest. In fact, it produces unrest! We have to trust in God's Word and be confident in his ability and not our own. We must recognize that He enables us to live victoriously through faith. We must separate ourselves from any areas of unbelief and choose to believe God. If we are believing God, we will live obediently to His Word and His instructions. Obedience to God and His Word gives us access to His rest. The door of faith is open to us; we have only to enter in.

*Connect to Rest*

## Matthew 11:28–30

*Father, forgive me for unbelief and disobedience. Cleanse me from every area of rebellion against You and Your Word. I turn from my own way of being right and choose to step into the rest that You have provided for me. I ask for help to follow the way of faith and obedience. Open my ears to hear You and obey You. Soften my heart to hear Your voice and walk in faith. In Jesus' Name, Amen.*

# Day 51

Read: *Joshua 1:1–9*

*"Do not be terrified or dismayed (intimidated), for the LORD your God is with you wherever you go."*

## "Steps of Faith"

God gave Joshua a guarantee that he would be with him. God knew Joshua would experience opposition in his new position over Israel. He knew that there would be many opportunities for fear and intimidation to stop Joshua's progression. Joshua was to remember that God was with him and to forge ahead with the plan of God, no matter what! The assignment God has given to each one of us is not without a challenge! There will be many opportunities for our enemy, natural and spiritual, to threaten, intimidate, and even brutalize us. All this is done for the sole purpose of stopping God's plan of prosperity and success for us. Opposition from all sorts of places will arise; however, God has already prepared the way for our sure success! We have to go forward in courage, like Joshua, and take what God has promised us.

We can learn from this passage of scripture that success is not without struggle or opposition, but victory is ours because God has promised to be with us in the things He has ordained. Be mindful though that the way forward is based on the promises of God, and not our own pipe dreams and agenda. If we will follow the will of the Lord, and what He has planned out for us, He will give us the victory as he did Joshua. Joshua followed God all his days, fulfilling the will of the Lord. If we practice this same principle, God will be with us as we fulfill all His will. Take the steps of faith and forge ahead to victory!

*God is Reliable!*

## Hebrews 10:23

*Father, faith pleases you, and I want to live and walk by faith. I repent of drawing back in fear and intimidation. I choose today to be courageous and forge ahead in obedience to Your promises for me. I take hold of the Truth that You are with me. I will not be fearful, timid, and cowardly. I forge ahead in faith, trusting that You are with me! In Jesus' Name, Amen.*

# Day 52

Read: *Philippians 1:6*

*"He that has begun a good work in you will ..."*

## "Make the Finish Line"

Starting and stopping can be a common thing for most of us. We start exercising only to fall off the wagon by not practicing the discipline that it takes to be successful. We begin a healthy eating regimen or diet meal maintenance plan, but soon get off track with one night out to dinner. We can even start bigger projects like college and, for some, not complete the four years required to graduate. We can start house projects and leave off completing the tasks because we never had the skills to complete them in the first place. Let's face it, we have all started and stopped something at one time or another.

It is good to know that in this walk with the Lord, He is committed to us to finish the work He began in us! We only have to be still long enough for God to work in us and on us. We should remember that *"all things are working together for a good outcome if we love God and are living for His purpose"* (Romans 8:28 paraphrased). His purpose and plan differ from ours, therefore we must look to Him for direction and guidance for life in Him. We should never attempt to align God with our will. Let us instead comply with God's plans and let him finish the work He began in us. God is expecting us at the finish line of the life He predestined, and He knows exactly how to get us there!

*God is effectively working!*

## Philippians 2:13

*Father, finish the work You have begun in me! I yield to You and Your agenda for me. Let me be cooperative and obedient to You in the process of my transformation into the likeness of Your Son. I want to finish strong, and You know how to get me to victory! Victory is what you have ordained for me, and I want Your success for me. My goal is Your finishing line! In Jesus' Name, Amen.*

# Day 53

Read: *Deuteronomy 16:16–17*

*"And they shall not appear before the LORD empty-handed."*

## "Bring a Gift"

Life is but a brief moment in time, and before we know it, we can be out of time. Our life and the duration of it is fleeting. We do not know when God will call any of us home. We do not know the day, nor the hour; however, scripture teaches that we ought to be ready on the day we meet Him. We all have a divine appointment with the King. The Maker, the God who created all things, and those very same things holding together every world system there is, will meet each one of us on an appointed day. Here in this passage of scripture, at the Feasts of Booths (Tabernacle), all the males, three times a year, were to go up to appear before the Lord. They were not to show up empty-handed but were to bring an offering that reflected the blessings the Lord had given to them. This made the gift measurable in the sight of the Lord.

As I prayed today, Deuteronomy 16:16 came to my mind regarding my own meeting day with the Lord. I said, "Lord, when my life is over, and I meet You, I do not want to appear before You empty-handed. I want to bring a life to You that is thankful and appreciative of what You have done for me. A life that has acknowledged Your deliverance and protection over my life. I want to present a gift to You, my King, that is reflective of the many blessings I have received from Your hand. I want my gift to matter to You!" So, to be ready, I asked my King today what He would have me do with the rest of my life to please Him, honor Him, and present to Him on our meeting day! Because, I refuse to show up empty-handed!

*The time is now to prepare for the King!*

## 2 Corinthians 6:1–2

*Father, I do not want to appear before You empty-handed! I want to bring a life lived for You, that is filled with purpose and acceptable fruit. You have loved me and blessed me abundantly. You have delivered, protected, and provided for me while here on this earth. I want my life to reflect gratefulness, thankfulness, and appreciation for what You have been to me, done for me, and given to me! I acknowledge the blessings! Today, I look to how I can prepare for my divine meeting with You. Holy Spirit, help me prepare, with the rest of my life, a gift that will please the King! In Jesus' Name, Amen.*

# Day 54

Read: *Matthew 22:36–40*

*"The whole Law and the (writings of the) Prophets depend on these two commandments."*

## "It Takes Two"

There are lots of dos and don'ts in the Bible. There are so many instructions to heed and obey. We can try to do them all, but none of us will succeed. God knew that we could never succeed in fulfilling all those commands, so He sent Jesus. Jesus allows us to live under grace for all the things we cannot measure up to heeding and obeying. Asking for forgiveness for our sins and our inability to obey every instruction is necessary for all of us. We need the grace that the blood of Jesus affords us. Every one of us needs the grace of God whether we recognize it or not. We need the free gift of God to not be sentenced to death, which is the penalty for sins according to God's Word. Following every single law is impossible. However, God still expects obedience to His commands, and He has given us two commands that will help us fulfill all the commands. *"Love God, and love others as you do yourself"* (Paraphrased).

We have to be sure of going in the way of love, and 1 Corinthians 13 gives us the description of what the right way to love looks like. Love here shows that we are to put others before ourselves. Operating in love takes the focus off of self and places it on the well-being of other people. Whether those people are worthy of love or not, we are commissioned by God to live a life that practices the biblical way of love. There are a lot of I's in 1 Corinthians 13, but the I's are what we ought to do in relation to other people, and what we ought to be doing based on God's Truth. Our relationship with God, and how we treat others, is how we fulfill all the law. It takes these two, loving God and loving others, to fulfill all the law. We must strive for perfection in love to meet God's goal in fulfilling His law.

*Love never fails.*

# 1 Corinthians 13:8

*Father, trying to do everything You have commanded seems to be impossible. I fall short in many areas. You said all the law and the prophets hang on two laws—loving You and loving others. I will strive to fulfill these two commands in excellence. You have said that love is the excellent way in 1 Corinthians 13. I want to walk in excellence according to Your Word. Loving in a biblical way is a goal You have set for all of us. I pray for fruit to manifest abundantly in these two areas. In Jesus' Name, Amen.*

# Day 55

Read: *2 Kings 19*

*"I will put My hook in your nose and My bridle in your lips and I will turn you back by the way you came, O king of Assyria."*

## "What Did God Say?"

Sennacherib, king of Assyria, was a bully to Israel. In the previous chapter of 2 Kings 18, Hezekiah, king of Israel, refused to submit to the Assyrian's power and, therefore, provoked Sennacherib to try and take Israel through fear and bullying tactics. The invasions of the Assyrian army on surrounding nations were absolute. The Assyrian conquest, and the invasions of Sennacherib, were well known to Hezekiah. Bullies can cause fame to themselves by word of mouth. Fear of someone's name and their fame to invade, crush, and subdue is all another nation may need to surrender without even a single act of resistance. Here in this passage, we see that the bullying tactics by the Assyrian king did not make Hezekiah surrender and give up before the battle even began. Instead, in the face of the Assyrian bully, Hezekiah sought the Lord, and prayed to God about what Israel was facing.

The enemy will try and bully us as people of God. We have spiritual enemies and natural enemies that will try and get us to submit to fear and intimidation through bullying tactics. When we see that a situation is more than we can handle, and it seems like we are outnumbered, we too must seek God and His counsel and wisdom. God is our defender and deliverer from difficult situations. We need not fear bullies and their intimidation tactics. God has the final say in every outcome of our lives, and He alone is able to bring victory in impossible situations. The Assyrian king departed, and returned to his own home just as God informed Hezekiah he would. There, while worshipping, King Sennacherib was killed by his own people. God always has the final say, no matter what it looks like. When bullied by the enemy, pray and seek God and what He says! We have a God who is all powerful, even over our enemies.

*Under pressure, operate in faith.*

## 2 Timothy 1:7

*Father, help me to have hearing ears to Your voice and what You have spoken to me in times of distress. Help me to rid myself of any voice that speaks contrary to You and Your Truth. Lord, show me how to rely on You in impossible situations and give me wisdom to make wise choices according to faith. Fear, intimidation, and bullying tactics from the enemy will drive me to pray and not to run and cower in timidity. In Jesus' Name, Amen.*

# Day 56

Read: *2 Kings 20*

*"There was nothing in his house or in all his realm that Hezekiah did not show them."*

## "Start Well and End Well"

Just because we start out well in life, does not mean we will end well. Hezekiah obviously had prayer power with God. His prayers were powerful! Death had come, but Hezekiah prayed and moved God to allow him fifteen more years of life. However, what took place after this is terrible! God, of course, knew what was best when He made the decision to end Hezekiah's life. God knew what the outcome would be and tried to prevent what would come. We can look at it this way, or we can ask, did Hezekiah take the opportunity God gave him and mess it up?

*"Pride always goes before a fall"* (Proverbs 16:18). That's scripture! Hezekiah's pride led him to show everything that was in his house to the king of Babylon. Say, show off! When we become arrogant, puffed up, and filled with pride, it causes us to make mistakes in our decisions. We can lead an exemplary life of piety and service for many years, only to have our reputation destroyed by some foolish display of self-importance. Hezekiah lost his way! When the word of the Lord came in verses 16–18, Hezekiah didn't even bother to seek the Lord and pray concerning the fate of the people or his children. His concern was only for himself, and the fact that he would not be around to see their destruction and captivity. Hezekiah did not end his life well. Hezekiah finished weak! His pride led him to make an awful mistake! We must keep God at the center of our lives and use our prayer power for the will of God and the benefit of others. Psalm 62:10 says, *"If riches increase, set not your heart on them."* Remember to start well, and end well!

*Keep your heart pure!*

## Psalms 62:10

*Father, teach me to number my days. To be wise in how I live from day to day. Holy Spirit, reveal to me any areas where pride exists and I make the mistake of trusting in riches and in myself! All I have is from You! Let me never forget that it is You that should be worshipped and glorified. Help me to keep my heart pure and to walk in humility as I fulfill Your will for my life. Lead me to pray not just for myself but for the well-being of others. Let me live for Your glory and not my own. In Jesus' Name, Amen.*

# Day 57

Read: *Isiah 41:10–13*

*"I will help you!"*

## "Victory in the Struggle"

God is not surprised by the difficulties we face, and He promises to give us what we need to get through our struggles. He is always aware of the challenges we face around every corner of life. What is going on in our lives—plans, plots, and evil motives of people around us, and the schemes of our spiritual enemies to defeat us—is no new news to God. Envy and jealously by forces of darkness comes with the gift of God on our lives. We are not to worry, be moved, concerned, or in fear about such things. God strengthens and hardens us to difficulties, and He promises to give us His right hand of justice and victory. We must keep our focus on God and His power to get us through any difficulty we face. We are to put our trust in God and His plans for us and remember that God is with us even in the presence of our enemies. He has promised to give us the victory in the struggle!

*The Lord gives the victory!*

## Deuteronomy 20:4

*Father, life is filled with difficulties and struggles. You know each one that I face and will face. I ask for Your courage to face each one in faith, believing You have given me victory in each one! I bind the spirit of fear from operating in my life, and I put on love, power, and a sound mind! I realize I may not like problems and difficulties, but they are a part of life. Help me to remember that You are with me in every struggle. Help me to remember You will give me the victory in whatever I face. In Jesus' Name, Amen.*

# Day 58

Read: *Mark 1:16-39*

*"Let us go on to the neighboring towns, so I may preach there also; that is why I came (from the Father)."*

## "Designated Vineyard"

We see Jesus, in this passage of scripture, in Galilee calling the disciples to follow him, casting out demons, healing the sick, and preaching the gospel. Jesus was fulfilling his reason for being sent to earth. He had an assignment to fulfill, and we see here that he was doing what he was sent to do. We too have a purpose for being here. God has divinely ordered a path for us to take to complete our individual tasks here on the earth. We see that Simon (Peter), Andrew, James, and John were fishermen, but when Jesus called them to follow him, they immediately left their occupations and followed. Becoming a disciple of Christ involves believing, trusting, and following his example. It will require us to leave our current situations to follow the path that the Lord has set for us. We must immediately leave all and follow Jesus to live a life of obedience to God's design and purpose for us. There is a set path that we must all fulfill to complete our life's work. Jesus knew his reason for coming, so he was able to follow and fulfill the Father's will. He cast out demons, healed the sick, and preached the gospel. This was why he came!

There is a very important message from this passage, a key point. We will be required to leave everything and leave immediately to follow Jesus! Remember that the work that God has for us will require our all. We must move into God's designated vineyard for us. If we bind ourselves to someone else's vineyard, we will lack the time, energy, and even the inclination to work in the vineyard God has planned for us. We are to live life making improvements to what God has given us to do. Living life with purpose in God's designated vineyard!

*Take your cross.*

## MATTHEW 16:24

*Father, You have a particular work for me to do. I pray today for Your help in re-evaluating my priorities. Help me to see the path of life You have set out for me. I have a purpose for being here, and I need Your help, guidance, and strength to move into that divine purpose! Lord, plant me in the right vineyard! You want the glory from my life, and I need Your help in fulfilling all Your desires. Holy Spirit, lead me and help me to pick up my cross and follow Jesus. In Jesus' Name, Amen.*

# Day 59

Read: *Hebrews 1:1–2*

*"Now faith is ..."*

### "Using Faith"

Using faith requires action on our part. Our faith is released by praying, saying, and doing whatever God instructs us to do. *Praying* invites God to get involved in our problems, situations, and circumstances. Praying for grace to go through things with a good attitude and putting on conduct that is pleasing to God is an expression of our faith. Admitting our need and dependency on God also demonstrates faith in God's ability and not our own.

*Saying* what God says through his promises is a demonstration of faith. Talking with a believing tongue works in our favor. Speaking with expectant, faith-filled words works in our favor and helps us to hold fast to a positive confession of faith! We can then pray with faith-filled words and an expectation for breakthrough and answered prayer. Words of faith and confidence are released with power and authority into the atmosphere. We will have what we say!

*Doing* whatever God is asking us to do through faith and obedience is key to our victory. Doing without seeing the evidence demonstrates my faith and trust in God! God may even ask me to do nothing! I have to follow this instruction in faith and obedience too. We can stand still and see the salvation of God when necessary! God wants us to be people of faith, and we must actively use our faith in praying, saying, and doing! Let us use our faith daily and see the power of God released!

*Let us produce works of faith!*

## James 2:14

*Father, Your Word says faith without works is dead. I pray today for faith to be active in my life through prayer, a positive confession, and acts of obedience. It is impossible to please You without faith, and I do want to please You. Let me not just hear Your Word, but obey it through a constant prayer life, a positive confession based on Your Word, and acts of obedience to instruction! Help me, Holy Spirit, to use faith by my actions! In Jesus' Name, Amen.*

# Day 60

Read: Acts *25:1–12*

*"The Jews who had come down from Jerusalem stood around him, bringing many serious charges against him which they were not able to prove."*

## "Unfavorable Circumstances"

As Christians, we want to live life in favorable circumstances. We feel, with God on our side, how could we lose anything or be subject to anything that would harm us. We most times feel that the devil is behind every unfavorable circumstance we encounter. However, that is not a true picture of what it costs to be a disciple of Christ. Here in our scripture for today, Paul is facing injustice and a plot and plan by the people that was designed to kill him (Acts 25:3). Paul is taking a stand for the Lord, and his stand could cost him his life!

As we stand for the Lord doing what He asked of us, it may not land us in safe surroundings. Our witness for God may not take us before people that like us, but rather hate us and desire our downfall. However, just as Paul stood for the Lord and faced threats, evil plots, and injustice, we too must be willing to face unfavorable circumstances for the sake of the kingdom. We may find ourselves in situations that have been the plot of someone else's hatred of our love for Christ! Remember, God will be glorified even by our persecutions! We have to be ready and willing to bear faithful witness to the Lord no matter the injustices we face, the hatred we receive, or the vicious plots set up by man. God is on our side as we stand for Christ! We are to be courageous and bold like Paul, enduring our own cross for the sake of the gospel!

*Stand up!*

## Ephesians 6:11

*Father, so often I do not want to face unpleasantries! I want things to be smooth and favorable for me! I want everything to go in my favor, and I want to be favored! This attitude is not based on Your Word and is not an accurate example of the life of a true disciple. I repent of an attitude of entitlement! I ask for forgiveness today for a lack of faith and courage! I put on the full armor of God today and take a stand for righteousness, regardless of the injustice I am facing now or will face in the future. I choose to bear witness to the Name and Person of Jesus Christ. Persecution will come, but I choose to stand for the kingdom! In Jesus' Name, Amen.*

# Day 61

Read: *Philippians 2:1–5*

*"Do nothing from selfishness or empty conceit (through factional motives, or strife)."*

## "Competition Divides"

Competition has no place in the body of Christ. Competition divides and promotes self, self-centeredness, self-aggrandizement, selfish motives, and self achievement. When we compete with one another, it places us in a space to want to be better than someone else. We are not in a game or competition with one another as brothers and sisters in Christ. We are not supposed to compare ourselves with each other, but rather be the best person we can be at what God has given us to do. We are to celebrate others and their abilities and accomplishments. We are to encourage others and build others up, and be willing to help others be successful. We are to rid ourselves of envy, jealousy, and competition! We as believers are to be unified with one another! We are to have unity in the body of Christ, not the evil desire to promote ourselves.

Let us practice the command to love one another by not thinking more highly of ourselves than we ought to, but rather by humbling ourselves in our own estimation and lifting others up instead. This is the example that Christ left us, and he wants us to follow it. Let's face it, Jesus was not in competition with the Father, or the Holy Spirit. The Father, Son, and Holy Spirit worked in unity together as One!

*Do not entertain envy!*

## GALATIANS 5:26

*Father, teach me to celebrate my brothers and sisters. Show me any areas of envy, jealousy and competition that I might be harboring within me. I repent of comparing myself with others. I choose today to work in unity with others and be a blessing to my brothers and sisters in Christ. Teach me to work with people in the body or for the benefit of the kingdom. I do not want to be an island unto myself, but a working, serving part to the body of Christ. In Jesus' Name, Amen.*

# Day 62

Read: *Esther 1*

*"And let the king give her royal position to another who is better and more worthy than she."*

## "Don't be Replaced"

This is the story prior to Esther's reign as queen, and Esther becomes *"the better than she."* Vashti was replaced because she was a queen that would not comply with her king. Vashti was not faithful to the position she possessed. There is a scripture that states, *"He who is faithful in a very little thing, is also faithful in much."* Here we see the unfaithfulness of the queen to the position she had been given. We have to be faithful in the things we already have. Vashti proved openly to be unfaithful and because of her position as queen, it was determined that the rebellion she exhibited would infect the entire nation. Our personal rebellion and disobedience have social and positional ramifications. How are we influencing the people around us with our rebellion and disobedience to our heavenly King? Rebellion and disobedience are like leprosy, they spread and infect others.

We must be willing and obedient servants to our Lord. No matter what is going on around us, we must not be participants of rebellion and disobedience to the Lord. If we find ourselves in this position, we are to immediately change our behavior, especially if we are people that hold positions of authority. We are to practice humble submission to the Lord. When he calls us, we are to answer and follow his directions, even if we do not agree with his instructions. If we do not, we run the same risk that befell Vashti. We can be replaced, and a better and worthier person chosen in our place.

*Remain Faithful!*

## LUKE 16:10

*Father, the desire to give up and go another direction is strong some days! This is an area of rebellion and disobedience, and I need Your grace! Forgive me for not wanting to come when You call, do what You ask me to do, and go where You tell me to go. I recognize that not doing what You ask is rebellion and disobedience, and I repent and ask for cleansing from my wayward heart and mind. Enlarge my heart and give me the capacity to obey your instructions and run in Your way!*

# Day 63

Read: *Esther 2:1–17*

*"And Esther won favor in the sight of all who saw her."*

## "The Beauty of Compliance"

Esther is the fulfillment of Esther 1:20. She fits the description of a better selection than Queen Vashti. Esther was chosen not only for her beauty, but for her obedient, compliant spirit. Esther was drafted into a process of finding a new queen. This process was not of her own choosing, nor one she sought after. However, Esther found favor with Haggai, the keeper of the women, and she found favor with King Ahasuerus. Esther was forced to make compromises in order for a greater priority to be carried out and fulfilled. Esther had to be faithful to that greater priority.

How do we handle situations that require compromise? Do we comply with the process or resist and rebel against the places we find ourselves in? There are many times that we are forced into situations that we did not choose, nor seek after. We are forced into positions that we would rather not be in and would rather not have to face and endure. Like Esther, by God's leading of course, we must submit to the process and plan of God for our future. Learning to submit—and allowing processes to stretch, strengthen, and mature us—yields the beauty of compliance to a greater priority.

*Submit even to human institutions.*

## 1 Peter 2:13

*Father, so often I am resistant to situations I am in. Especially those situations that are unjust, and difficult to endure. I admit I don't like it! I feel taken advantage of, and view my situation through eyes of negativity. I resist the process and make things harder for myself. I recognize today that I need to repent and turn away from my own way and comply with the process You have placed me in. While I may not see the greater priority, help me to submit and be compliant with the process for Your will to be carried out.*

# Day 64

Read: *Lamentations 3:39–42*

*"Let us test and examine our ways, And let us return to the LORD."*

## "Revival in Me"

We as believers have to be determined to leave things in God's hands. This can be difficult when going through problems and situations that are beyond our control. However, the ultimate solution to our problems can be found in God. Turning to God with a contrite heart is key to revival. Constant acknowledgment of our own sins and shortcomings requires our repentance and return to God. There is relief in our own personal revival, and that revival begins in us. Our heart's cry must be, "Lord let the revival begin in me." The relief and restoration of repentance lies in coming back to God! We must test and examine our own ways and once again turn to the Lord.

Lifting up our hearts to God in prayer brings God into our problems. He will hear and answer our prayers and restore us to a right relationship with Him. While the problems and unpleasant situations may not yield an immediate change, we can be changed while going through them. Our hearts can be strengthened, encouraged, and revived! This will give us a different perspective and outlook on what we are facing. We then begin to use faith and trust in God as our strategy to combat our problems, and He can do anything but fail! We can leave the issue in His capable hands, and we can watch Him work things out for our ultimate good!

*God will work it out*

## Romans 8:28

*Father, today I begin again to seek Your face in the midst of the problems and situations I face. These issues are more than I can bear and more than I can handle. I know that You are able to handle all my problems and to work each one of them out for my ultimate good. In reflecting on my own ways, I realize I have tried to handle things on my own. Today, I repent and turn from doing things my way. I look to You, Lord, acknowledging You as my help. Revive my heart and mind today! In Jesus' Name, Amen.*

# Day 65

Read: *1 Peter 2:11-17*

*"Keep your behavior excellent among the (unsaved) Gentiles (conduct yourselves honorably with graciousness and integrity)."*

## "Be Seen"

What stands out today in this passage of scripture is the admonition to conduct ourselves in a manner that reflects our Christianity. We are to live as servants of God at all times. We are to show respect to all men and treat people with honor, regardless of how they may act or what they may do. As servants of God, our conduct is to be proper. Proper conduct according to God's standard is to act honorably and righteously before people. Our good conduct is a witness to Christ and the life he has instructed us to live. We are to live in a way that makes an impact on others. When we live godly lives before others, it brings honor to our God. It is a visible witness to God, and it brings Him glory.

If we fear the Lord, we will have respect for him and his laws. We will live in obedience to the best of our ability. Our love, respect, and honor for him will lead us to want to do right and act with honor. How we conduct ourselves matters to God, and it should matter to us. We must be a witness to God through our conduct. Living epistles for Christ is an effective witness because people see us before they hear us!

*Be a letter from Christ.*

## 2 Corinthians 3:3

*Father, thank You for the strength to be the witness You have called me to be. Let Your Holy Spirit live through me and help me be an example of the life of Christ. Lord, I ask for discipline to live godly before all men. Let the words from my mouth, my actions, and my character be not only acceptable in Your sight, but in the sight of all men. In Jesus' Name, Amen.*

# Day 66

Read: *1 Peter 3:8–15*

*"He must search for peace, (with God, with self, and with others)."*

## "Relational Maturity"

Living in harmony is not what people practice. Every person has their own personality, and we practice exercising who we are. Very rarely are people trying to live peaceably with others. Pride in us demands that we demonstrate who we are and what we want. However, people of God must practice living in peace and harmony with others. The balanced life of Christ in us will enable us to practice living in harmony with people. There are ingredients we need to cultivate to get along with others effectively. Developing sympathy, compassion, humility, peace, and a careful guarding of the tongue will help us cultivate this ability. Cultivating relational maturity is how we gain peace and harmony with God, and with others. We are to actively pursue peace and harmony not just with ourselves and God, but with other people. Christ in me brings peace to me. Christ working through me will bring peace with others around me. Peace working around me will yield the fruit of harmony with other people. The scripture tells us not to just desire this peace and harmony, but to actively search for it. Let us be active in relational maturity.

*Bear the fruit of maturity.*

## GALATIANS 5:22–24

*Father, cleanse me of pride today! I ask for Your help to cultivate a heart and mind of harmony within. Holy Spirit, let the mind of Christ work effectively in me and through me. Teach me to work peace within and without. I humble myself today to the mind of Christ and His nature and character. Help me to set a watch over my tongue and to develop sympathy, compassion, peace, and humility with others around me. In Jesus' Name, Amen.*

# Day 67

Read: *1 Peter 5:1-7*

*"Shepherd and guide and protect the flock of God among you."*

## "Honest Sacrifice"

For those of us that are leaders in the church, we are to be builders of God's kingdom, not kingdom builders for ourselves. Our hearts as leaders must be towards God and His genuine love for his sheep. Otherwise, we will handle the sheep wrong! We will not have a right kind of love for his sheep and will use them rather than nurture them. Pastors and leaders after his heart require us to promote the sheep, not ourselves.

Helping and supporting others is not just for leaders. We all are to be Christians that help support and promote others. This is being like Christ. He came here to bear the sins of man so that we could regain access to the Father. This pleased God! Christ's sacrifice for our benefit was pleasing to God. Jesus is our example for how we are to think and act. The Lord wants an honest sacrificial life for others. Do we sacrifice ourselves for others, or do we sacrifice others for ourselves and our own agendas?

*Be interested in others.*

## Philippians 2:4

*Father, so often I am thinking only of myself. I repent for selfish motives and any hidden agendas I might have, knowingly or unknowingly. Your example is to be concerned about others, not just myself. Help me to change in this area. Let Your mind be in me, and Your example be ever before me. In Jesus' Name, Amen.*

# Day 68

Read: *2 Peter 3:8–18*

*"Since all these things are to be destroyed in this way; what kind of people ought you to be?"*

## "Protect Your Image"

As the scriptures tell us, Jesus Christ is surely returning. God's goal to transform us into the image of His Son, by His power, is His number one goal for us as Christians. Our personal conduct is a major factor in God's agenda for us. We are to be spotless and blameless. This agenda is not the world's goal for us. The world cares nothing for how one lives, acts, or thinks. The work of grace, the knowledge of God, forgiveness, and transformation is God's personal agenda for us. These godly characteristics must be worked in us before God can work these things out of us. Bearing the fruit of godly character is pleasing to God and a visible sign of our Christian walk.

We are to walk out this Christian faith we have and become more mature and developed in godly wisdom and character. Our eyes must always keep the focus of growing up in the things of God. We must mature and strive for the holy lifestyle God wants and expects us to live. We need to be found by Him, upon His return, living a life of obedience to His will and purpose.

*Diligently live for Christ!*

## Philippians 1:21

*Father, I ask for Your help in living godly. Help me to mature in the nature and character of God. Help me to put away childish behavior and put on godly wisdom. Instruct me in Your Word and help me to apply what I learn. Give me understanding and discipline to live holy and acceptable before You. In Jesus' Name, Amen.*

# Day 69

Read: *John 6:1–14*

*"There is a little boy here who has five barley loaves and two fish; but what are these for so many."*

## "Participate by Faith"

Here in this passage of scripture is one of the miracles of Jesus. Jesus told the disciples to feed the people, which was five thousand individuals. He requested that they take care of the problem. The disciples recognized that they did not have food to feed all those people. We can learn something about Jesus and His expectation of us to participate in the miracle that meets the needs of others. There was not enough, and Andrew basically says we do not have what we need. This is a type of unbelief. However, Jesus demonstrates that He is able to take what we do have and bring increase to it to meet the needs of others.

It is by faith that we can please God. It is by faith that we believe God can take what we have to offer and meet the needs of the people that we encounter. Our faith must rest in the power of God and His ability to multiply what we have and solve the problem of someone else's need. If we pull our gifts, talents, and resources together, Christ's power upon what we bring to Him works miracles to bless others. The Holy Spirit uses what we have and works a miracle for the sole benefit of the needs of others. What do we have to give to meet someone else's need, and are we willing to participate by faith?

*Let your faith rest in the power of God.*

## 1 Corinthians 2:5

*Father, I want to participate by faith in meeting the needs of others. Lord, show me what I have to offer to help meet someone else's need. You are the miracle worker, and I know You want to continue to work miracles on the earth. Help me to be a willing vessel to continue Your miracle-working power for the sole benefit of others. I believe You are able to multiply and increase whatever I have to bless others. I offer You my gifts, talents, and resources to be used for miracles! In Jesus' Name, Amen.*

# Day 70

Read: *Philippians 2:13*

*"Not in your own strength."*

## "Rise Up"

Christ leads us to victory; if we will continue to follow Him, we will get there. We are to be diligent in following His instructions and carrying out His will. Any challenges, trials, and tribulations that we encounter, God promised to work for our good. We are to keep His purpose in the forefront. We are to not allow our hands to be slack in the service and work of the Lord. We must not contribute laziness, unproductivity, and slothfulness to the work of God. He expects us to be productive in our efforts to serve Him.

The hope and blessing that we have is that while we must rise up and do, God is the power and strength that enables us to do it! He promises to arm us with His strength and give us the creativity, power, and desire to do what He has instructed us to do. We, however, must be willing to get up and work out the plans and purposes that He has given us. There will be opposition to our promised land, but God has given us the victory to obtain what He has promised. He will do it for His own good pleasure, satisfaction, and delight!

*God gives the strength, the power, and the desire!*

## Psalms 18:32

*Father, help me to keep and uphold Your purposes in the forefront of my life! Lord, lead me to fulfill Your desires and not my own; grant me discernment to know and see the difference between the two. Strengthen me to choose Your desire, and to work and add the things that contribute to Your purpose and plans. You have promised me victory in reaching places You have promised to give me. In Jesus' Name, Amen.*

# Day 71

Read: *Matthew 4:18–22*

*"Follow me and I will make you fishers of men."*

## "Empowerment Makes, Exploitation Takes"

Jesus took twelve men and made each one great! Jesus used their occupations, gifts, and talents and made them great men for the kingdom. Jesus empowered these men! Jesus used what they had, and what they knew to make them great men for God's kingdom. When you empower someone, you give them authority and power to do something. You enable them and make them stronger and more confident, especially as it relates to their own life. Empowerment sets people free to live in liberty and freedom and carry out what has been put on the inside of them by God for His glory and the furtherance of His kingdom.

Exploitation, however, takes people's gifts, talents, and skills and makes full use of them for gain and benefit. It is selfish, and it uses people and capitalizes on what others possess. Exploitation takes! It does not empower, but rather seeks to take what others have and put it to good use. There is a big difference between empowerment and exploitation. Great leaders empower people, and Jesus is our example. Weak leaders exploit people, and we must be careful to keep ourselves free from exploitation. We all need to be people that empower others. Nobody wants to be exploited, and that is not the example that Jesus left us. Let us not seek to make ourselves stronger on the backs of others, this is exploitation. Let us instead empower others by encouraging, strengthening, and *helping to make* others stronger!

*Empowerment liberates!*

## JOHN 8:36

*Father, thank You for the liberty that You have given to me through Your Son, Jesus Christ! He died so that I could be free to love, serve, and live for You. Let me be discerning when others would exploit me rather than empower me to be all that You have made me to be, for Your kingdom. I recognize that all that I have belongs to You. Every gift, every talent, and every skill is Yours! Lord, lead me, and guide me to people that would empower me and help me to be great for You! Your kingdom is important to me, and I want to be all I can be for Your glory! Teach me to empower other people and not to use people for my own purposes and agendas. In Jesus' Name, Amen.*

# Day 72

Read: *Luke 6:31–36*

*"He is kind and charitable and good to the ungrateful and the selfish and wicked."*

## "Mirror, Mirror"

Is our character working for us or against us? How do others see us? Are they drawn to us or is there an aversion to us? What is our believer presentation to others? God expects us to exhibit character that looks like Him. So often, we think we get a pass on how we act because we have accepted the gift of salvation. We are born-again Christians walking in the Lord and living the kingdom life! Hallelujah! Well, we don't get a pass on behaviors that are not in keeping with the message of the cross, which is love! We see in these verses of scripture that we are to mirror the love of God to others, even others who do not have loving behavior.

Demonstrating the love of God to those that love us and to the unlovable is being like our Savior and Lord. It is the message of the Father and His will for His children's character, nature, and behavior. Mirroring the love of God is practicing mercy, tender-heartedness, and the compassion of Christ, in whose image and likeness is God's. We too have been re-created in Christ's image as the children of God. Let's remember to practice and mirror God's love in all things and towards all people!

*Own it, and wear it!*

## Colossians 1:12

*Father, I recognize that my behavior does not always exemplify Christ-like character. I repent and ask for forgiveness for acting in some other fashion besides the one that You have instructed in Your Word. Thank You for forgiveness for my shortcomings and my ungodly behavior. I am so glad that where my sin abounds, Your grace abounds even more! Holy Spirit, help me to be like Christ not just in word, but also in deeds. In Jesus' Name, Amen.*

# Day 73

Read: *Deuteronomy 3*

*"For you shall not go over this Jordan."*

## "Know No"

Are we willing to accept God's no, as well as His yes? Oh, it is wonderful when all His promises are yes and amen to us! When God answers our prayers with a positive resounding yes, we shout, we praise, and we honor Him with our thanksgiving. However, what happens when God's answer is no? There are times that God says no to a prayer, a request that we may have or have believed for. When those times come and God answers no, what is our reaction? How do we feel? Can we even imagine Moses' disappointment and hurt over leading Israel out, but not being able to lead them in? How devastating that must have been to Moses. What a disappointment to not be able to share in the blessing of entering the promised land that he was used to bring the Israelites out of Egypt to inherit. We see here that God is saying no to Moses and Moses has to accept God's no.

We must identify where God is saying no to us. Our heart, mind, and will, will want to forge ahead of God and push past His no as an act of faith! However, believing God is not an opportunity to practice faith to obtain our own agendas. Believing God is having faith in His plans, His purposes, His desires, and pushing to fulfill those agendas. God's agenda is different from ours, and in those seasons and times that God says no, remember Moses, and learn to accept the no. It will be uncomfortable, yes, difficult, and maybe even heartbreaking, but there are those that have gone before us that have been told no too. In a real and true relationship with the Father, He doesn't just say yes, He also says no.

*Nevertheless!*

## LUKE 22:42

*Father, I get so used to expecting Your positive, resounding yes. Lord, I know that yes is not always what's best for the things that I ask and believe for. Help me to grow up and be willing and able to accept a no from You. This will take maturity on my part, and a willing and receptive heart to Your will. Help me to be okay with a "nevertheless." Let me be able to go on in joy to the no's that You will have to give me sometimes. I love You. In Jesus' Name, Amen.*

*Day 74*

Read: *Jeremiah 23:16–21*

*"Do not listen to the words..."*

## "Great Expectations"

We as believers are here to fulfill God's expectation for our lives. There are so many other things that vie for our time and attention. We tend to carry out the dictates of these other things and can find ourselves pursing things outside of what God intended for us. There is no greater distraction to the plans and purposes of God than people. These people can be family, friends, spouses, relationships, clergy in the church, and even our children. We must keep God's will and expectations for us at the forefront of our lives. Trying to fulfill people's expectations and what they want and require can be a life lived under tyranny. We are obligated to fulfill what other people want and need rather than what God is telling us. We must let God determine our values and behavior patterns, and pursuits. We must be mindful that Jesus changed people, they didn't change Him! He fulfilled God's expectation for His life despite the voices of other people.

We must always seek God for clarity on our lives and do what He expects of us. We must not allow others to control us and dictate our lives in a way that bears no fruit, brings no joy, and fulfills no purpose for what God intended for us. Unfortunately, here in this passage of scripture, these people can even be those that shepherd over the sheep. God's expectation is greater than that of other people. God is the one who will give out the reward, and that reward will be for fulfilling His expectations, not someone else's!

*Aim at and seek*

## COLOSSIANS 1:3

*Father, so often I am pursuing either my own desires and expectations or someone else's. Both these pursuits are wrong. Lord, help me to fulfill Your expectations for my life and Your goals for my life. I understand in this moment that only what I fulfill for You will bring me the reward in heaven that's given at the end of my walk with You. Today, I shut out all the voices of man's expectations from any avenue in my life that is keeping me from serving You and fulfilling Your expectations on my life. In Jesus' Name, Amen.*

# Day 75

Read: *2 Corinthians 6:14–18*

*"For what partnership have right living and right standing with God with iniquity and lawlessness?"*

## "Living Healthy"

As we grow in our Christian faith, we want to be wise in who we spend our time with. We must cultivate and pursue healthy relationships. Relationships are not healthy if one person is in control while the other struggles for approval. While we want the fellowship and companionship of others, it is better to be lonely sometimes rather than be controlled and manipulated by the people around us. We must especially be aware of our relationships with unbelievers. Relationships influence our actions and behavior. We must begin to cultivate new godly relationships with believers that are walking in God's Truth. Godly relationships help us to be strengthened and encouraged in our Christian walk.

The scripture that tells us to not be unequally yoked is not just for marriages, but for all of us as we seek to cultivate relationships that are godly and healthy as well. We must make alliances consistent with our faith and remember that two must walk together in agreement. As we yoke ourselves together, even with other believers, the relationships must be ones that keep us free in the liberty that Christ has given us.

*Walking healthy!*

## Amos 3:3

*Father, as I continue to walk in the faith, give me eyes to see the relationships in my life as You see them. Help me to weed out relationships that are controlling and manipulating my life in a negative way. Give me opportunities to meet and fellowship with other believers that are walking in the liberty that Christ died to give us. Lord, help me to cultivate not only godly relationships, but healthy ones as well. In Jesus' Name, Amen.*

# Day 76

Read: *Ephesians 5:20–24*

*"Strip yourselves of your former nature."*

## "Inside Out"

The Bible tells us that the heart of man is wicked and deceitful, and that God is the only one that knows the heart and mind of man. As we walk in faith, we must take time to look at the things that are corrupt on the inside of us. So often we spend a lot of time looking at the outer sins in our lives, and the sin and iniquity of worldly behavior. However, our heart and mind are secret places that wickedness and iniquity hide themselves in. God looks at the hidden man of our heart and rewards us accordingly!

Keeping the mind of God in our hearts and thoughts takes discipline! There are keys in the Word of God to help us obtain and hold to the mind of God. If we do not pull the reins of our minds in, we will keep the shape of the unregenerated self which is characterized by our old nature's corrupt and sinful ideas, thinking, ways, and behavior. We must assess and reassess daily the mind of the inner self. If we do not, we will remain stuck in the life of our old man. Our minds and hearts must be renewed daily, and the former self with its wickedness must be put off and the new nature in Christ adopted. This transformation must take place daily, and even our minds and hearts must be scrutinized by the Truth of God's Word. The hidden man of the heart must be cleansed daily for holiness to manifest in our lives. Let us not forget that holiness is God's goal for His children, and this holiness is to work itself inside and outside.

*Take time to inner-self clean!*

## Jeremiah 17:9, 10

*Father, "Create in me pure heart, and renew a right spirit within me." Holy Spirit, open my eyes to see the hidden man of my heart and what needs to be cleansed today. Lead me to daily spend time in Your Presence and help me to see areas where there is hidden sin and iniquity. I thank You for forgiveness of sin and the restoring blood of Jesus Christ. I thank You that You alone know my heart and love me enough to reveal sin in it that I might be able to repent and ask for forgiveness. In Jesus' Name, Amen.*

*Day 77*

Read: *Job 10:2-8*

*"Show me why You contend with me."*

## "Making Greatness"

Dark seasons of our lives are confusing when we are walking through them. Fiery trials, developing our gifts and making us stronger, are farthest from our minds! Let's face it, we question God, just as Job did. Our faith is most obvious and tangible in times of trouble. God knows this, and therefore He allows us to go through some things, some very tough things! Faith must be tested, and our gifts cultivated. Without the fiery trials of our suffering, we remain unaware of the gifts we hold and the faith we possess! As we learn to appropriate God's grace in our suffering, we learn to depend on Him. We grow in our recognition of His power and ability to help us in our time of distress. God helps us realize that He alone can help us overcome, go through, and endure the trials we face.

We have to recall that when we go through fiery trials, God is not trying to kill us. He is rather shaping us into the image of His Son. We must remember in these times we are to stand in the fiery trial, holding onto God's arm of Strength! He wants to be the one that brings us through, so that He alone gets glory for Himself out of our lives. We will need to let our spiritual legs be developed and grow to have an ability to stand! Our faith will be perfected and shine brighter, our hearts and minds will be transformed in righteousness, and our level of compassion for others will grow and mature. God is creating in us the image of Jesus, and the end result in us will always be one of greatness!

*Soldiers stand tall!*

## 2 Timothy 2:3

*Father, I admit I do not like fiery trials. However, the Word of God says my faith must be tested and that I must be able to go through and endure hardship. Help me to recall this truth when in the fire of trouble and struggle. So often, I do not see or understand this truth while going through life's struggles. Holy Spirit, help me to remember God's hand in the fire! Lord, give me an ability to stand in faith in Your ability to bring me through any difficulty. In Jesus' Name, Amen.*

# Day 78

Read: *Genesis 20:33*

*"But Abraham remained standing before the Lord."*

## "All-Knowing"

Our reading tells us *all* the men from the city surrounded Lot's house. This is an indication of the widespread evil of the city. *All* the men of Sodom were wicked and depraved. God knew there were not fifty, nor even ten, righteous people in Sodom. However, we see that God allows Abraham to reason with Him on the destruction of the city. God allows us to stand before Him and reason as a friend, as a son, as a daughter. We can talk to Him about situations and issues that we see and have knowledge of. We can question Him respectfully, and even disagree with His decisions.

We may see a situation one way and talk to God based on what we see, feel, and think. However, God knows every situation from beginning to end. He knows the details of everything! He knows the hearts and minds of men everywhere! He knew that all of Sodom was depraved and wicked, and that was the reason for His decision to bring destruction in the first place. God knows what He's doing even if we do not! At the end of our reasoning, talking and praying about things we feel strongly about, we have to respect and trust God's decision, even the decision to bring destruction on a people, a thing, a situation, and even on a person! He is an *All-*Knowing, Righteous God!

*Accept His righteousness!*

## Psalm 145:17

*Father, often I have thought Your decisions were harsh. I have not understood why You have chosen to do certain things. I have not agreed with outcomes and have been angry and offended! Father, forgive me for my attitude and the condition of my heart about life in general! I repent for being offended by Your Sovereignty! Holy Spirit, help me, and remind me that God is Righteous and Holy, and He knows what is best in, and for, every situation. I thank You, Father, that I can talk to You and pray to You and reason with You as a friend, but at the end of it all, You Reign and Rule over all things! In Jesus' Name, Amen.*

# Day 79

Read: *Isaiah 40:31*

*"Shall change and renew their strength and power."*

## "Vibrancy Restored"

There are often times that we as Christians get off the track in our walk with the Lord. Life, and its responsibilities, begins to take our focus and our strength. We lose power, our passion and our relationship with God become secondary at best. We have lost our position and have become stagnant. We need to get back on track and reposition ourselves back in the place of resting and waiting on the Lord. How do we reposition and get back to a place of vibrancy and power? We must begin to swim upstream. We must begin to do things differently to make a change.

Every one of us, as Jesus' disciple, has an assignment. We each have a piece of the whole that we are responsible for. Jesus trained His disciples and released them. They did not all stay in the same place, nor did they all go to the same place. Jesus sent them out to spread the gospel. Jesus' style of leadership did not realign His disciples to an organization, rules, or programs. They were called to a personal relationship with Him. They were given the choice to follow Him each day. Our journey with the Lord is inward in relationship and outward in public ministry. The closer we get to Him, the more He moves us outward in serving others. We must always realign ourselves to this pattern that Jesus gave us in our journey with Him. This is the pattern that makes disciples, and it restores us to passion, vibrancy, and power.

*Come to Jesus*

## Matthew 4:19

*Father, so often I find myself off track and out of sync in my walk with You. It is my prayer today to realign myself with You and Your agenda for my life. You know the way for me to go, for You have already prepared it. Lord, by Your Holy Spirit help me to reposition myself to the pattern You have designed for my assignment. I look to You today and refocus on my relationship with You. I thank You that as I focus on You, I will be changed, renewed, strengthened, and empowered! In Jesus' Name, Amen.*

# Day 80

Read: Galatians 5:4–5

*"Through the (Holy) Spirit's (help), by faith anticipate and wait for the blessing and good."*

## "Help to Hope"

There are seasons in our lives where we feel bad about our walk of faith. Our days are so darkened that we cannot see anything good before us. Our situation looks hopeless, and we find ourselves without faith and hope to believe God! In our knowledge of God and His Word, we know that as Christians, hopelessness is the wrong way to walk! However, life can put us right here. Well, this is not as hopeless a situation as it appears. God reveals to us in His Word that we need the Holy Spirit's help to wait in faith and hope for the blessing of good that He promises us as righteous believers. We are to rely on God's help to even wait on Him to hope.

There will be dark hours and seasons in our lives as Christians. We can take comfort in knowing that when it is so dark that we cannot see a positive outcome or victory in where we are, we are okay to wait on hope from the one that gives more hope. The scripture says that *"faith is the substance of things hoped for."* Remember, when you are feeling hopeless and feel your faith has failed, wait on the God of Hope to restore hope to you and the situation you face. Patience in waiting on God for hope will give us the divine power we need to believe again!

*He is the God of Hope.*

## Romans 15:13

*Father, I thank You for Your Word today that has taught me that there will be times that I feel hopeless. That trials and suffering will come to me in a way that I can see no hope, and my faith will fail. Help me, Holy Spirit, to remember to look up and to ask for help to wait for my hope to be restored and faith to rise in my heart again. Lord, help me to recognize that as the God of Hope, You can and will restore hope in me so that I can once again walk in faith, believing and trusting You even in the darkness. In Jesus' Name, Amen.*

# Day 81

Read: *Matthew 7:24–27*

*"So, everyone who hears these words of Mine and acts on them, will be like a wise man."*

## "Foundations of Obedience"

Often times, we blame God for our painful or difficult circumstances. This is especially true when we do not understand the outcome of our circumstances made by our own acts of disobedience. There is a law of reaping and sowing that we fail to attach to circumstances and events that leave us devastated, broken, and feeling betrayed by God. Our cries of woe, anger, and betrayal do not allow us to hear the voice of God and His wisdom concerning the circumstance. In reality, if we would hear God, He would show us the mistake of not listening and obeying His Word. We make a choice that is one of disobedience, and then we lay that choice on the foundation of Christ. We then expect everything to work out in our favor, and that blessings will be ours. Then when life turns south, we become angry, hurt, disappointed, and hopeless! We cannot make a choice of disobedience to the Word of God, then put that act on the foundation of Christ and expect success.

The scripture in this passage tells us that to obey the Word and do what it says bring protection, and success, but disobedience to the Word of God is stupid, and will result in failure. We must own our choices and take responsibility for our actions of disobedience to the Word of God. Sometimes these actions can be small but yield big, fat failures that leave us bewildered! Repentance and responsibility will go a long way in this walk with God. It will open our eyes and understanding to see and hear Him tell us exactly where we went wrong! This is even His grace and mercy towards us to correct us and tell us our faults. It is not always easy to hear either! However, when we hear His correction, we must own it and take responsibility for the circumstance that we have blamed Him for! I repent, Lord, is the only thing we can say to turn things around and begin to move forward! Healing can begin, and we will begin to grow again in maturity, repentance, respect for God, and faithful service to Him. Our foundation must be one of obedience to result in success.

*His love reveals our faults*

## Revelation 3:19

*Father, I thank You for Your grace, mercy, and forgiveness. I stand in need of all today as I reflect back over some of the choices I have made. Lord, I repent for choices made that were disobedient to Your Word. I repent also for blaming You for the outcomes of those choices. Lord, teach me to make right decisions and choices that reflect the kingdom and its agenda. Help me to grow up and take responsibility for my own actions, and to walk out the results of bad choices with grace and dignity. In Jesus' Name, Amen.*

# Day 82

Read: *Matthew 3:14*

*"And he appointed twelve to continue to be with Him, and that He might send them out to preach (as apostles or special messengers)."*

## "Disciple through Relationship"

The closer we as believers get to the Lord, the more He moves us outward into serving others. Jesus came to serve, and He demonstrated this service to us through His example. However, Jesus also had a relationship with His disciples. Out of His relationship with them, He then modeled service to others. His small-group method of relationship and then discipleship is the vehicle Jesus used to teach, train, equip, and release His disciples to change the world!

We are all both disciple and disciple-er. But we must not forget to build relationships with people as we teach, train, and disciple them. There are people we can teach and train, and then there are people that can teach and train us. We must model this small-group way of discipleship and pray for this process to multiply. There is a successful process to making disciples. Teach, train, equip, and release. However, let us not forget to build relationships as we disciple others and are discipled ourselves.

*Make disciples using the right pattern.*

## MATTHEW 28:19

*Father, help me to fulfill the great commission of making disciples. Lord, teach me to use the pattern that You used in Your relationship with Your disciples. Let me not forget to build relationships with the people You send me to disciple, and the people sent to disciple me. Relationship was important to You, make me mindful of this example, and help me to follow it as I am sent out to multiply the kingdom of God. In Jesus' Name, Amen.*

# Day 83

Read: *2 Corinthians 9:8*

*"And God is able to make all grace (every favor and earthly blessing) come in abundance to you."*

## "Alpha and Omega"

The work that God gives each one of us is specific to us as individuals. He has designed us and purposed us in an assignment that He has already prearranged. This means that He also provides for the work that He assigned us. We must seek the mind of God to carry out the work that He has given to us. We require His instructions and guidance to execute the plan He has for the work.

The work originates with God, the plans come from God, and the completing of the work ends with God. Time spent with God is necessary to complete the work that He has given us. Without seeing Him for instructions for how to move forward with what He has given us, we will never be able to walk in our service for Him for the benefit of other people. All things begin and end with God, even our life's work and service!

*All God!*

## Philippians 1:6

*Father, I need to repent first for not wanting the work You expect of me and planned for me to complete here on earth. I am sorry for the apathetic attitude I've had towards what You've given me. Cleanse my heart and mind, and forgive me for a lack of passion concerning Your plan for me. I ask forgiveness also for not recognizing that all things begin and end with You! That You are the provision for everything, especially the very thing You have purposed for me to do here on earth! Lord, Your kingdom come, Your will be done, through me here on earth as You have ordained for me in heaven! In Jesus' Name, Amen.*

# Day 84

Read: *2 Corinthians 9:8*

*"God is able to make all grace (every favor and earthly blessing) come in abundance to you."*

## "Sufficient in Christ"

God's desire is that we would be self-sufficient in Him. We must remember that when God calls us to do something for Him, He is well aware of our inability to accomplish the task. In fact, it would appear that when He speaks to us about an assignment, He does so when we are absolutely inadequate for the job! This is on purpose, for He has designed us to find the adequacy to fulfill His will, in Him! The Lord provides for the work that He has given us, but the sufficiency to accomplish His will comes from nothing and no one else but God!

We must remember God is able to multiply our resources to complete the work that He assigns us to do. We are not to approach what God gives us to do in our own strength, and dependent upon our own resources. His grace is sufficient for whatever we need to complete the work He assigns us. We can be sufficient in Him for every good work.

*God is able!*

## Ephesians 3:20–21

*Father, I repent for thinking I can do things all on my own. I know that apart from You, I can do nothing! You are my Sufficiency and all that I need to do Your will comes from You. You provide the resources for all that You have given me to do. It is by Your ability and not my own that anything gets accomplished. All glory belongs to You! In Jesus' Name, Amen.*

# Day 85

Read: *Jude 24, 25*

*"Now to Him Who is able to Keep you without stumbling or slipping or falling..."*

## "In the Deep End"

Life and various circumstances can make us feel overwhelmed, and that we are in over our head. However, God is our strength; He has control of our lives, and He is never in over His head! He is able to keep us safe, and we are upheld by His grace. We must remember that without God, we will always feel in over our heads. There are many things in this life that can leave us bewildered and paralyzed by the trauma of fear, suffering, loss, disappointment, and shattered hopes. We can be left feeling confused and without direction for our next move forward.

The stepping stones to our successes is to choose the life that God has carved out for us. At every fork in the road of life, we must take responsibility in trusting God, even when things do not make sense. We must reach down deep and find the courage to press past fear, mistakes, mistreatment, and the injustices of others. All of life's challenges will present things to push us into fear and the fear of failure, but in those times, remember that God is in the deep end of our lives, and He is right there with us to keep us!

*He is there!*

## Joshua 1:9

*Father, thank You for the promise of being there with me no matter where I am! I will not fear but, by faith, put my trust in You. You have promised to keep me from stumbling, slipping, or falling. I will trust You to keep me as I walk through life knowing You are able to uphold me and lead me to places of victory! In Jesus' Name, Amen.*

# Day 86

Read: *Matthew 14:22–36*

*"Take courage, it is I! Do not be afraid!"*

## "Courage to Obey"

Courage is the opposite of fear. To do something in the face of fear and danger is to have courage. We must be able to take some chances and live on the edge when the Lord bids us to come. We have to listen and obey, and to be so connected to Him that we step out to do what He commands us to do. Peter obeyed when Jesus bid him to come. Can you imagine, Peter actually got out of the boat! That was courageous of Peter, and it was a bold move for him to step out of that boat onto a stormy sea. Peter took courage and obeyed the Lord, and he walked on that water with the Lord, until he took his eyes off the Lord. Once Peter lost his focus, he began to sink!

There is a clear message here for all of us that want to live life with courage and boldness. We must be people of faith, not in ourselves, but in God! We must believe that whatever He calls us to do, He is there to keep us walking upright and sure-footed. We must constantly keep our focus on Jesus to live boldly in life and remember that whatever God gives us to do in this life, it will be a water-walk journey! The way forward will be impossible without our courage to obey, and the power of God to keep us!

*Courage is a discipline.*

## 2 Timothy 1:7

*Father, thank You for the power that is able to keep me. Holy Spirit, help me to take courage in what the Lord is calling me to do, and where He may be calling me to go. Lord, help me take courage and do all that You planned for me to do in this life. I declare that You, Lord, have not given me a spirit of fear! I declare that I am full of courage and boldness to obey God! In Jesus' Name, Amen.*

# Day 87

Read: *Psalm 51:1-13*

*"For I am conscious of my transgressions and I acknowledge them."*

## "Heart Monitor"

David, according to scripture, was a man after God's own heart. This kind of heart must be cultivated, developed, and maintained. David followed the Lord, and when he made mistakes through sin, he confessed his sin and turned away from them. It was not David's sinless life that endeared him to God, but rather his transparency and ownership of his sin and wrongdoing. It is better to own our sins rather than make excuses and try to cover them. God already knows that we err; in fact, He knows even before we carry out wrongdoing that we are going to err.

In following Christ, we have to will ourselves to go after Jesus. We have to be willing to deny ourselves the prideful comfort of blaming someone else for our sin and expose it as our own transgression. Ownership of sin is crucial in being open, transparent, and honest with God. We never have to be ashamed of wrongdoing. However, we are to acknowledge, confess, repent, and turn away from sin. God is so willing to pardon us when we are sincere about repentance. Our heart needs to constantly be monitored. We must allow God to cleanse, purify, and restore our heart to a right position before Him.

*A heart for God.*

## 1 Samuel 13:14

*Father, thank You for Your Mercy and Grace to forgive sin and iniquity. Make me to know sin in my heart and mind that I might repent and turn away from my transgressions. Forgive me, Father, for missing the mark often. In Jesus' Name, Amen.*

# Day 88

Read: *Matthew 10:35-42*

*"And he who does not take his cross (expressing a willingness to endure whatever may come) and follow Me ..."*

## "Life Choice"

Pursuing the life of Christianity requires that we let go of the life that we currently possess. We all work so hard at obtaining things from this world's system. We pursue jobs, houses, education, relationships, and much more, seeking to obtain success here on earth. However, scripture teaches us that it is losing one's life in this world that puts us on the path to the life that Christ suffered to give us. In a word, it's summed up in "sacrifice." Instead of grasping for the wants and needs of ourselves, we are to consider the wants and needs of others. Living our lives not just for ourselves, but with the needs of others in mind.

Jesus taught us the concept of dying to oneself and pursuing the desire of the Father through His death on the cross. He told us that there was no greater love than to lay down one's life for a friend (John 15:13). In pursing Christianity, we must make a life choice to live daily for the benefit of others. Like Jesus demonstrated, we are to pursue sacrificial living. We need to remember that the sacrifice will cost us our "I, my, and me" way of living. We must understand that the self-life the world promotes must be laid down, to please the friend we have in Jesus.

*Love in action.*

## John 15:13

*Father, I need Your Holy Spirit to help me on a daily basis to choose the life You died to give me. Teach me to pursue a life of sacrifice to please You. Let me learn to give back to You the glory of a life lived for others rather than a life lived for my own desire and pleasure. You have promised me that if I pursue You and the kingdom of God first, You will give to me everything else. In Jesus' Name, Amen.*

# Day 89

Read: *2 Corinthians 11:3*

*"But even as the serpent beguiled Eve by his cunning, your minds..."*

## "Mind's Desire"

The mind can be beguiled, corrupted, and seduced from wholehearted, sincere, and pure devotion towards Christ. Prayer is needed for ourselves and for others. We must cover our minds in the word of Truth. While we might be in fellowship with the Father, we too, as Eve was, can be deceived into breaking fellowship with God through the doorway of seduction and deceit. Knowing God and being in relationship with Him does not protect us from the spirit of deception. Our minds are to look like the mind of Christ. This is a mind with an attitude of humility. It's the mind of servitude. It's a mind that seeks to fulfill the desire of the Father rather than pleasing the desire of ourselves. It's a sacrificial mind that desires to obey God and His will. The deception we will always face and fall prey to is the mindset that seeks to fulfill selfish desires. We are deceived when we choose the way of self-gratification over and outside the will of God.

*Mind attitude.*

## Philippians 2:5

*Father, I pray for the mind of the Spirit. I pray for life truth and the integrity of an attitude that seeks to please You. Forgive me for leaning on my own understanding instead of the wisdom that comes from obedience to Truth. Help me to do Your will and seek to serve You and Your Word. In Jesus' Name, Amen.*

# Day 90

Read: *Proverbs 16:18*

*"Pride goes before destruction."*

## "Struggle through Prayer"

We can all find ourselves in difficult situations. The natural thing to do is try and figure things out on our own and try and take matters into our own hands rather than to trust God for the answers. Scripture tells us to cast our concerns on the Lord because He cares for us and is concerned about us. This can be cliché when we are in the clinches of a real problem. It will take a humble approach when faced with hard places. We must take the way of prayer and seeking God and His will rather than allowing pride to take control and try to run the show.

We can only change ourselves in any difficult situation. Learning to lean on God and His strength is the only sure way to balance our faith with proper, effective actions. It is best to go the way of dependence on God rather than depending on our pride to figure things out. Remember, it will be the way of pride that causes us to struggle in difficulty. Humility must lead us to a place of prayer and trust in God. Prayer will help us to hear God's instructions and change our focus from the problem to God's help. Prayer will help us to cooperate with the Holy Spirit rather than struggle in the situation through pride.

*Humble yourself and pray.*

## Philippians 4:6

*Father, forgive me for trying to figure things out for myself. Help me to humble myself and pray and seek Your face in all the problems that I encounter in my life. Holy Spirit, help me to remember that I can do nothing on my own, but only by prayer and the wisdom that comes from God can I overcome life's difficulties. In Jesus' Name, Amen.*

# Day 91

Read: *1 Timothy 1:5*

*"But the goal of our instruction is love."*

## "Love's the Main Goal"

When serving God as believers, we must have good works that give evidence to our faith. We are to add to our faith good works that demonstrate our faith. The works that we do must be purposeful in loving others. Our works need to operate along with our faith as we pursue daily obedience to please the Father. Good works cannot be a sideline to our Christian walk but must be the main thing we pursue in loving and pleasing God.

Love is what is important to God, and we are to be willing to change our focus daily to loving people through our good works. We must do the things that matter to God, and people matter to Him. The Father sent His one and only Son to give His life for mankind. It was the love of God that sent His Son, and it was for the love of the Father and man that Jesus died. Love is what was the motivating factor, and love must be what motivates us to do good and serve God and people.

*Love is the main directive.*

## Matthew 22:37–40

*Father, religion forgets about the well-being of people. Lord, lead me daily to live a life of love through good works towards others. Forgive me and cleanse me where I have fallen short and forgotten the main purpose of our relationship. Remind me daily to not only love You but to love others through my actions. In Jesus' Name, Amen.*

# Day 92

Read: *John 8:37*

*"My word has no entrance (makes no progress, does not find any place) in you."*

## "Free Indeed"

May we learn to love God in a way that honors Him and the love He has for us. Our freedom was purchased by the blood of Jesus, God's Son. His only begotten Son! It's this blood that has set all men free. All men were redeemed and set free and now have access to come before a Holy God. This freedom is for all, but we know that not all have accepted this or embraced this love from God. We must receive the freedom and accept it as our own. We must put a claim on what God has freely given to us.

The entrance of God's Word brings light, and we have to allow that Word to have an entrance into our hearts. The Word must be found in us for us to experience the free gift of freedom that the Father has extended to us. This is where free will and free choice come in. God will not make us receive His Word. We have to allow it to have an entrance into our heart! Will we allow the Word to abide in our heart, or will we reject Truth and become an enemy of the cross? Wisdom embraces the Word and lives a life of love towards God in return for the freedom He's given. Will we allow its entrance?

*Experience Freedom*

## JOHN 8:31–37

*Father, I pray that Your Word will have an entrance into my heart—to make progress and find a place within me. My freedom was purchased by the blood of Jesus, and I have been set free. I have access to You, a Holy God who receives me and accepts me! I pray that I experience the freedom You purchased for me by way of the cross. I am free indeed! In Jesus' Name, Amen.*

# Day 93

Read: *Romans 1:1*

*"A bond servant of Jesus Christ (the Messiah) called to be an apostle (a special messenger), set apart ..."*

## "Separated Life"

Paul, here in Romans, discloses what he is in Christ. He recognized that he was not his own, free to do as he pleased. He lets us know that in Christ he is set apart for a specific duty to the gospel of Christ. In 2 Corinthians 6:17 it says that we are to come out from among unbelievers and be separate. We are to be set apart for salvation and service to God. It is in the separated life that we demonstrate that we are the sons and daughters of God. Many proclaim to be in Christ, but the life of the true believer must exemplify the consecrated, and yes, set-apart lifestyle of the One that has chosen and called us for His purpose

A right relationship with God is one where He calls the shots. It is His will that must be supreme and of most importance to us. A life where we call the shots, make our own decisions, and do what we want and feel is not a life that is consecrated and set apart to God. We must relinquish control and give God control of our lives. He calls us to be set apart like Paul for His glory. Set apart, we live life according to His will!

*Separated for Him!*

## 2 Corinthians 6:17

*Father, thank You for the life in Christ that You have given to me. I receive Your free gift of grace and mercy! I in return give You my life for Your honor and glory. Holy Spirit, sanctify and set me apart, and help me to walk in the abundant life that was purchased for me. Give me strength to live the life that You have prepared! In Jesus' Name, Amen.*

# Day 94

Read: *Matthew 7:9–11*

*"How much more will your Father Who is in heaven (perfect as He is) give good and advantageous things…"*

## "Yes and No"

Do not have a bad attitude because God does not give you what you ask. We must trust Him to give us what is good for us, but we must also trust God's no. Learning to trust God for His yes and no calls for maturity. Children expect to get everything they want and ask for. Children are taught that you don't get everything you want when their parent tells them no. Natural parents want to give good things to their children, and that resembles a yes. When it's not good for the child, the parent says no. As children of God, our heavenly Father makes the same choices for us when we ask for things. We must remember God wants to give us good things, and we must trust that when he says no, it is for our good. Maintaining a good attitude in our yes and in our no times demonstrates our maturity in Christ, our trust in His decision, and our respect for Him as our heavenly Father.

*He works all things for our good.*

## Romans 8:28

*Father, forgive me for being angry when I don't get what I want or what I've been praying for. Help me to trust You for the answers to my prayers and requests. Help me to understand when You say no, that it is working for my good. Lord, forgive me for the lack of respect when I have not gotten what I wanted. I repent and ask for Your forgiveness. I want to be mature in Christ and grow up in love, honor, and respect for You as my heavenly Father. Let me learn to live with and be okay with Your no. Teach me Your way, O God. In Jesus' Name, Amen.*

# Day 95

Read: *Numbers 9:15–23*

*"In accordance with the command of the LORD ..."*

## "Specific Timing"

In reading this passage of scripture about the cloud on the tabernacle, we see that the Israelites moved at God's direction. As long as God's Presence was in their midst, they rested. When it lifted, they journeyed. God's Presence guided their movements. It was all about His timing and His direction. We can learn from this passage that we as people of God need to continuously look for God's direction. We have to learn to wait for God's timing and take our directions and instructions from the Holy Spirit. The Holy Spirit is our guide on how to move in God's timing. Listening and following God's direction teaches me to learn to obey instructions day by day. God does have specifics for His people. We need to practice listening, waiting, following, and moving according to God's directions.

*Submit to Gods directions.*

## Proverbs 3:5–6

*Father, lead me, instruct me, and direct me according to Your will and Your timing. Help me to recognize Your voice and show me how to move through life according to Your instructions. You have given me Your Holy Spirit to lead and guide me. Thank You that You have not left me alone to figure things out on my own. In Jesus' Name, Amen.*

# Day 96

Read: *Deuteronomy 3:23–25*

*"Enough! Speak to me no longer about this matter."*

## "Shut Up!"

In reading this passage, I was surprised at the Lord's response! God's Word tells us we may have to labor before the Lord in prayer by its teachings, and parables. I was reminded of the common saying that the Lord's delay is not His denial. I thought about all the feel-good stuff about persistence in prayer. I was reminded of the parable of the widow and the unjust judge that granted her petition because the widow was persistent. So, I was truly speechless after reading this conversation between Moses and the Lord. Truthfully, I didn't know where to begin to put together a daily devotional. However, here we go! Are we mature enough to hear God tell us to shut up! Can we handle God saying to us that He will not grant our request and, as a matter of fact, to stop speaking to Him about the matter? Is God still good in our estimation when He tells us no? Can we continue to love, serve, adore, and be loyal to a God that would tell us no to our deepest desires, our prayers, and our petitions?

Loving God will require us to be able to accept His no and continue our relationship with Him in trust, obedience and a good attitude! We cannot be in a relationship with the Lord to only gain what we want. There will be denials, and we have to be mature enough and in love with God enough to accept His no, and to stop talking to Him about the matter. In Luke 22:42, Jesus' request was denied. The cup was not removed, and He went to the cross. Simply put, are we willing to shut up about a matter after God says no?

*Request denied!*

## Luke 22:42

*Father, we don't even know where to begin to pray for strength, wisdom, and understanding in seeing and accepting Your ways. Forgive us for not being mature enough to accept Your denials. Help us, Holy Spirit, to discern when we need to accept the Lord's answer to a heartfelt petition. Help us to remain faithful when You have decided to say no to prayer requests and petitions. Help us to remain steadfast in our faith and loyal in our love and commitment to You. In Jesus' Name, Amen.*

# Day 97

Read: *Luke 15:11-32*

*"But the elder brother was angry (with deep-seated wrath), and resolved not to go in."*

## "Inward Prodigals"

When we read the parable of the Prodigal Son, the light is always shined on the younger son, who took his inheritance from his father and went and squandered it. He wasted all the money, became homeless, and was lastly eating with the pigs, an unclean animal to him and his heritage. Well, that is sad and terrible behavior by this son. The parable goes on to tell us of this son's epiphany and return home to his father's house, and the welcome and restoration he receives.

Today, I want us to look at the other son, the elder brother. I would like to say that both these sons were prodigal! The fact that the older brother stayed home and did what was right and expected did not exempt him from being prodigal. As believers, our religious conduct in doing what is good and right does not exempt us from the nature of a bad attitude! This elder brother's attitude was one of self-righteousness, self-importance, self-pity, bitterness, and resentment, to name a few. This elder brother had an attitude problem and his sins were that of the inner man. While the younger brother was guilty of sins of the flesh by riotous living, this elder brother's sins were hidden sins of the heart. The attitude about his brother's return and restoration was just like the Pharisees and scribes. The lost sinner, like his lost brother, was unacceptable to him. A bad attitude does affect our behavior. Harboring such things as anger makes us miserable people. Let us not just be concerned how we act on the outside, but let us keep our inward man sanctified and surrendered to the nature and character of God. Inward prodigal is just as bad as outward prodigal, because God sees our heart even when no one else can.

*How do I look?*

## 1 Samuel 17:7

*Father, I know that You are concerned about my inward man just as much as You are about my outward man. Lord, help me to give attention to my attitude and bring it into subjection to the nature of Christ. Holy Spirit, sanctify my inner man to be holy as God is Holy. In Jesus' Name, Amen.*

# Day 98

Read: *Psalm 37:7-8*

*"Do not fret; it leads only to evil."*

## "Don't Do It"

Here in this passage, it says that fretting is not something we should participate in. It is a definite admonishment to not allow ourselves to be emotionally unhappy, discontented, and worried. So how do we switch fret off and find an attitude of contentment, gladness, and happiness? The goal is to rest in the Lord instead. Resting in God does not depend on external circumstance at all, but on our relationship to God Himself.

When we find ourselves fretting in life, and usually fussing as well, we have entered into sin, and this is an avenue that leads us in the determination to have our own way. Fretting is an indication of anxiety and worry, which leads to the sin of not trusting God. It is not a position of wisdom, but rather wickedness. Jesus never worried and He was never anxious because He was not out to realize His own ideas. Jesus was out to realize God's ideas and His way in each circumstance He faced. Jesus' words in the terrible circumstances he faced were *"not my will, but thy will be done."* We too can put our supposing about situations aside and choose to rest in the Lord in trouble. We are to cease from calculating things without God through the avenue of fretting. Don't do it!

*Restore Your Joy, Lord.*

## Psalm 51:12

*Father, forgive me for fretting and worrying caused by my reasoning and calculating without You, Your Power, and the Truth of Your Word. I thank You for forgiveness and the grace in not giving me what my sins deserve. Cleanse my heart, mind, and attitude of thinking I can change my circumstances apart from You through fret. Lord, I choose to turn to You and rest in You alone! In Jesus' Name, Amen.*

## Day 99

Read: *Isaiah 35:3-7*

*"For waters will break forth in the wilderness and streams in the desert."*

### "Desert Streams"

The valley is where so many of us faint and give up! As we read this passage, we get a glimpse of God predicting the restoration of Israel through water manifesting in the wilderness. We never look for nor expect the blessing of refreshment in the dry and barren places of our lives. God shows us here that He is capable of showing up and making what appears to be fruitless and empty into a flourishing, prosperous, and blessed place!

The wilderness, and the dry places we find ourselves in at times, has streams and waters that break forth at God's command. God has a plan and vision for us, and He is not in a hurry to complete what He has begun in our lives. He does everything on His timetable, and He is working on us even in the barren places. He is always working us into the vision that He has predestined for us. We are not to lose heart in the dry places, but look for what God is doing in those dry places. Look for the streams in the desert that are the Father's handiwork! It is here that God chooses to move in the miraculous by creating desert streams.

*Do not lose heart.*

## 2 Corinthians 4:16

*Father, thank You for the blessing of renewal in barren places. Lord, I look to You as You make a way for me in the wilderness; refresh and restore my soul. I acknowledge You have a good plan for me, and my future is predestined for me as I walk with You. My soul takes refuge in You. In Jesus' Name, Amen.*

# Day 100

Read: *John 10:10*

*"I came that they may have and enjoy life, and have it in abundance (to the full, till it overflows)."*

## "Enjoy Life"

To have eternal life is great, but there is more. Believing brings eternal life, but Christ came so that we could have life to the full! All believers have life, but not all have abundant life. To have abundant life there must be continual fellowship with Jesus. Apart from Him there is no abundant life. The abundant life is found in Christ alone!

To possess the fuller life, the believer must abide in Christ (John 15:1–5). Everything is in Him! Without abiding in Christ, the Christian life becomes meaningless and mundane. If we do not strive for the abundant life that exist for us in the Person of Jesus Christ, we will soon yield to the life the world offers. This life is carnal and full of flesh and its appetites. The carnal life is circumstance driven. The abundant life is Holy Spirit controlled and designed to lead us in victorious living. We must determine to live God's best and to enjoy the life He has given to the fullest.

*Partake of the fullness of joy.*

## Psalm 16:11

*Father, thank You for the abundant life You provide through Christ. I accept Your gift of life and recognize that it is only in You that I can receive and enjoy life to the full and over-flowing! Holy Spirit, help me to abide continually in Christ Jesus who provides to all who believe, accept, and abide in Him the abundant life. In Jesus' Name, Amen.*

www.ingramcontent.com/pod-product-compliance
Lightning Source LLC
Chambersburg PA
CBHW071703090426
42738CB00009B/1645